From Recruit to Res
The 24-Month Guide to 9-1-1
Dispatch Center Excellence

From Recruit to Responder: The 24-Month Guide to 9-1-1 Dispatch Center Excellence

Cherie Bartram

This book is designed to provide accurate and authoritative information in regard to the subject matter covered. It is sold with the understanding that the author is not engaged in rendering legal, accounting, or other professional service. If legal advice or other expert assistance is required, the services of a competent professional should be sought.

Second Edition.

ISBN-13: 979-8-88955-606-0

Trademarks

For more information, visit www.equature.com.

I am dedicating this book to the life and memory of Karen Gregoric. She was an ardent supporter of public safety and the education of PSAP personnel at all levels. Thank you, Karen, for your passion, diligence and conscientiousness to your career and family. Gone too soon, truly missed by many.

CONTENTS

AUTHOR ACKNOWLEDGEMENTS

Authoring a book has been a goal of mine since I was a child. At only nine years old I would pretend to write books. At one stage in this development, I wrote a "book" by "rewriting" Little Women into Little Men. It had several chapters completed before other adventures grabbed my attention, but I found it so exciting to paint pictures with my words. When I was ten, I won a young author contest and was able to spend a full day at a local university in writing workshops and mentorship discussions and I loved it. Given this, my first acknowledgement is to my parents. Carl and Millie, without your never-ending support, encouragement, and love I simply would not be who I am today. You allowed me the freedom and opportunity to spread my wings and fly, preparing me with the ability to sharpen my pencil along the way in preparation for a time such as this. I love you deeply and I am honored to be your favorite daughter.

Along my journey in public safety, I worked with a variety of mentors. Each agency and organization held people with quality character traits and were where I wanted to be in life. They were stern, honest, insightful, and sometimes it was their actions and not their words that inspired me. To those agencies, Lakewood PD, Estes Park PD, St. Clair County Central Dispatch, SERESA and organizations, Michigan Communications Directors (MCDA), NENA Institute Board (NIB), National EMS Advisory Council (NEMSAC), I want to say thank you for your belief in me and especially for the opportunity to work for you and with you.

Specifically, in my journey, thank you to Hilda Carter, Heather McCarthy, Randy Repola, Mark Thorner, Mike Smith, Mike Holland, Harriet Renee-Brown, April Heinze, Dr. Bob Cobb, and Eric Parry. I know there are more and although I did not list you, each of you are in my heart and I will always be humbled by your positive contributions to my career.

I would be remiss if I did not specifically mention my current employer (Equature), who provided me with the platform to fulfill this life-long dream. Our visionary leader, Joe Mosed (and the sales team), Paul Frezza for his referral to the company, Heather Froom, Tiffany Chan, and Don Gillis (my editor). Thank you for your encouragement, guidance, support, and patience. Without you, this book would not have been possible, you have no idea how much this opportunity has meant to me.

My family at home and afar—the importance of your support is extraordinary. Your encouragement and patience while I locked myself away to "write my book" will always be deeply appreciated. My children from afar—the frequent calls and texts to see how things were going were very important to me. Matt for regularly calling me on your way home from work just to check in is awesome—I love those calls. Thank you so much. Still at home, Riannah and Nathan, so young and yet so supportive, not having me always available to help with projects, school, and play time might have been frustrating but you did a great job of showing me love. Roger, my husband, my best friend, for coming into 30 years now you have been by my side. There are not enough words to say how much you mean to me. Thank you for taking over the dinners, the kids' activities, and being a loving and supportive ear. You have my unending devotion and love.

INTRODUCTION

In the United States, the official emergency number for public safety, 9-1-1, became law in March 1973. This came after five years of enhancements and testing following the first 9-1-1 call in Haleyville, Alabama by Senator Rankin Fite who dialed those digits and was connected to Congressman Tom Bevill as he waited at the local police station. This was a big leap in the United States with advanced technology. In the 1960's and 1970's, households had "party lines" which meant they shared their home landline with at least one other household within the same area code. Obtaining a private landline meant more money, so budget conscious households would share the line, which included having to wait to use the phone if the other household was on it. It also meant that your line would ring busy for someone trying to call you if another party occupied the line. Eventually party lines, which often also included renting the actual telephone, were replaced by private lines and lower phone costs so consumers could buy their own hardware.

As telephones became more common across the country, fire departments advocated for a single, simple number easily dialed in the event of a fire or other emergency. The United Kingdom had implemented the concept in 1936 with 999. A big advocate in telephone growth in the United States came from AT&T (American Telephone and Telegraph Company). As the US moved forward with the one number concept, the Country worked closely with AT&T who suggested using 9-1-1 because it was easy to remember, and it had not yet been assigned as an area code or other designated number. AT&T became the "big guns player" when they bought out their competitor, Bell Telephone in 1899 and proceeded to purchase other smaller phone companies while maintaining the Bell Telephone name, often referred to as "Ma Bell". This was considered an allowable natural monopoly for phone service then because of the prohibitive cost of developing infrastructure for other carriers. Lasting until 1982 after an antitrust suit settlement between AT&T and the United States department of justice, AT&T split into regional operating companies (known as Baby Bells) until other companies began to emerge and supply a competitive market (such as Sprint and MCI). AT&T has diversified since then, along with dropping their telegraph service and adding Voice Over Internet Protocol (VoIP) and wireless technology.

The implementation of the 9-1-1 number changed the workflow for the Public Safety Answering Points (known as PSAPs). The introduction and worldwide adoption of mobile devices with 9-1-1 capabilities changed the workflow again creating a higher volume of incoming calls per incident and a public demand for better technology. The growing technology changes and job duty expectations, coupled with public perceptions of what 9-1-1 really is has impacted every aspect of public safety telecommunications as a career in both a positive and negative way.

CHAPTER 1

Why Choose Public Safety Telecommunications as a Career

The truth of the matter is that the call to become a 9-1-1 Professional is not a career that most people think of when listing off the topics of "what I want to be when I grow up." Even those in the profession who are second or third generation public safety servants may not have started out with the goal of working in a Public Safety Answering Point (PSAP). PSAP leaders must devise plans to attract the caliber of applicants needed to fill the seats with competent individuals dedicated to public service. The challenge to change the prevailing career path for 9-1-1 as a steppingstone profession is real. A quick Google search will show job openings in the 9-1-1 profession, highlighting that 9-1-1 can be the beginning of a public safety career where the applicant can "promote or advance" to law enforcement, EMS, or fire services. There is no question as to the depth of support for these other fields in public safety, but 9-1-1 is its own career. Moving to law enforcement, fire, or EMS is a career *change* not a promotion. The 9-1-1 career path can and is, its own path with a variety of areas in the 9-1-1 arena to keep professionals engaged for decades. Within the PSAP, there can be progression depending on the PSAP. Job classifications vary from PSAP to PSAP. The saying "you've seen one, you've seen them all" does not apply for any branch in public safety. If you have seen one PSAP, then you've seen one PSAP is the more appropriate statement. Given this, the task of selling a career in public safety telecommunications is not as much a matter of "why this career," but rather, "why not!"

The ability to attract and retain public safety telecommunicators is a challenge throughout the industry. Not only do PSAPs compete for applicants, but the private sector (referred to as commercial partners or public safety vendors) also offers appealing opportunities for individuals striving to make a difference in the industry. Low paying PSAPs may be able to hire and train individuals only to lose them to any higher paying PSAP within a 20-mile radius. The private sector can often offer higher pay, reduced stress, travel, a vehicle or in some cases a vehicle with a gas card, and in many opportunities the significant ability to be flexible. Competitors may also offer attractive recognition benefits that include annual cash incentives based on performance. With the average PSAP wages in the United States listed by salary.com as $43,000 ($20.67/hour) (Salary.com, 2022), PSAPs offering less in benefits can usually count on a high turnover rate as employees seek to better their financial status with exposure to more opportunities.

The Great Resignation

Staffing crises throughout the country have caused businesses to lower their standard qualifications, offer hiring incentives, tap in on the boomerang employees, and figure out what makes their enthusiastic stayers stay. In September of 2021, a record 4.4 million people quit their jobs with no reported signs of stopping until those buoyed by stimulus funds experienced a personal savings decrease and re-entered the labor force (Liu, 2021).

In 2010, Workplace Psychology (Nguyen, 2010) reported that the top 5 reasons employees stay at an organization are:

1. Pride in the organization - People enjoyed working for a well-managed organization.

2. Compatible supervisors - People stated they wanted to work for someone who is supportive of them.

3. Compensation – People wanted fair and competitive wages and benefits, as well as opportunities to gain experience and achievements.

4. Affiliation - People wanted to collaborate with colleagues they respected and liked.

5. Meaningful work - People enjoyed working for companies that let them do work that appealed to their passion.

But those motivating reasons have shifted over the past 10+ years according to ForzaDash. Digital fatigue is real, and employees are craving an emphasis on relationship building more than ever. Employees in the workforce today list their top reasons they stayed at an organization as (the top 6 are included to show a trend change):

1. Compensation - Employees base their value on a specific salary amount. Well-paid employees are said to be more motivated to work, stay productive, and become more loyal.

2. Mentored - Employees appreciate mentoring to teach them the trade. Without a strong mentoring program, employees can experience being overwhelmed and demoralized.

3. Challenged - Employees want challenging work, not the same routine every day. They want to be stimulated to do better.

4. Promoted - People want to have opportunities to move up in an organization. It gives them confidence and sense of value when recognized and rewarded for their work.

5. Involved - Employees want to be involved in company processes and operations. It makes them feel important, needed, and boosts their morale (Pannone, 2019).

6. Appreciated - Employees want to know that the organization appreciates them for what they do, which motivates them to do better.

Given this, in February of 2022, a survey of 6,627 adults (Parker & Menasce-Horowitz, 2022) found that the top three reasons given in the United States for why employees quit their jobs were:

1. Low pay (63%)

2. Lack of opportunities for advancement (63%)

3. Feeling disrespected at work (57%)

Those surveyed stated that these listed areas were the *major* reasons why they left. Other surveys conducted revealed that most managers lack the top qualities employees want in a boss, providing a whopping 82% of workers consider quitting because of a bad manager (Brady, 2022).

The desire for challenges and recognition has soared with today's workforce and while some of the top reasons are similar, the current workforce is looking for a little more—something those who have been in leadership for a few years must recognize. Employees want a knowledgeable boss they can depend on, competitive pay, advancement, and respect for them as a person. This is a shift for both current and future employees and included in changes to a hiring process along with incorporated into daily operations.

Job Descriptions

The job descriptions within a PSAP may include positions or advancement in the following areas:

- Call taker

- Dispatcher

- Lead Dispatcher

- Communications Training Officer (CTO)

- Quality Improvement (Lead, Supervisor, etc.)

- GIS Specialist

- IT/IS Specialist

- Supervisor

- Operations Manager

- Deputy Director

- Director

However, not all PSAPs are the same and not all will have these opportunities for advancement. This leads us back to the original question and the title of this chapter—Why Choose Public Safety Telecommunications as a Career? When recruiting for an opening, remember to list the top motivators for a career, such as:

- Career Advancement

- Making a Difference

- Helping People

- Benefits (includes insurance, retirement, and wage compensation)

When reading the top motivators, were you wondering why "making money" was not listed at the top? A career in public safety telecommunications is hard. It taxes you emotionally and physically and if money is a motivator for your applicant, this may not be the career they are looking for. While compensation is important for attracting and retaining PSAP employees, money alone is often no enough. The challenging nature of the job—with rotating shifts, weekend and holiday work, high call volume, and office politics—can outweigh financial incentives. However, some applicants may be passionate about public safety and drawn to the tight-knit 9-1-1 community. For these individuals, serving the community becomes more important than the salary. Though pay remains a consideration, it is no longer their top priority. Focusing on creating a positive and supportive environment that is appealing to an applicant's sense of purpose may be a more effective retention strategy than pay alone.

When I was 19 years old (going on 20), I moved away from my home state and all that was familiar for me to the State of Colorado, 1300 miles away because I was tired of small town living and everyone knowing my business. I knew I needed a J.O.B. with benefits, money, and insurance. I applied at every local government that was hiring. In 1983, it was not as hard to keep the PSAPs staffed once training was complete, and I was raised to believe that a government job, at any level, was stable and safe. I was familiar with public safety, having worked for an ambulance company for almost 2 years, so that became my focus, but I was not fully prepared for the 9-1-1 environment. The first 9 months were rough, but I stayed because it was a solid and fulfilling job (and I am exceptionally stubborn). Nine months turned into five years and there was a point that I wished I did not have to work. By that age, I was married with one toddler and another baby on the way. My sick time usage went up and my attitude went down. My agency had a part-time option that saved my career. For three years I was able to work in a position called temporary part-time pool and fill overtime openings while being a mommy. I worked a little every week and filled in the last-minute overtime openings. It was a perfect blend of family and career. When I went back full-time, I had a new outlook. Within two years, I applied for an opening at my dream spot in Estes Park Colorado (ironically a small town where everyone knew my business) and was fortunate to be hired at that agency. From there, my career soared and it was no longer a J.O.B. I realized then that I had been bit by the public safety bug years prior and I had found my niche.

Career Advancement

Applicants often ask about career advancement and may go in search of other opportunities if the PSAP they are applying at does not appear to offer the opportunities for advancement they desire. When speaking to applicants, remember that for telecommunicators (dispatchers), once trained, there are areas for one to get involved and to develop a long and fulfilling career. Those who have successfully passed a training program and probation may wonder what is next, and the answer is look around! Everywhere we look in our jurisdictions, there are civic groups who would love to have a 9-1-1 presentation for schools, youth groups, convalescent care staff, banks, mall security personnel, elected officials, and even first responders not working in the PSAP. Truly the list is endless because each of these groups of individuals would find that a presentation on 9-1-1 would fill a void of information that they may not even be aware of.

Public speaking is not their thing? There are organizations writing and re-writing best practices. Always eager for volunteers, APCO and NENA are just short emails away. States often have a variety of committees to get involved with such as training, technical, and oversight committees. There are national programs and training available to take one's knowledge to a higher level. The National Center for Missing and Exploited Children offers advanced training for telecommunicators and a plethora of tips for those with young children through the teen years. There are organizations throughout the country looking for champions to improve Cardiac Arrest survival in their communities, an effort that begins with the 9-1-1 call and telecommunicator CPR, or T-CPR as it is known. Another important association is TERT - The Telecommunicator Emergency Response Taskforce. TERT is a nationally recognized training curriculum for telecommunicators and leaders who want to be considered for an activation response during a disaster deployment or to assist with another TERT PSAP during a critical event. The APCO/NENA ANS standard was developed to address the added training and responsibility needed for TERT responders. You may find more information on the TERT program under the APCO/NENA ANS1.105.2-2015 standard.

That is great, but what about inside the PSAP? Moving up the career ladder is a familiar process. The advancement is designed to formally progress an employee to a higher level of job responsibility within his/her current position. When thinking of advancement, people often only think of this type of latitude, hence the phrase, "climbing the corporate ladder," so make sure every opportunity, horizontally and vertically, in the PSAP is highlighted in the application process.

Levels of Responsibility

Carefully review the variety of levels of responsibility you have in your organization. There are levels that require formal documentation and informal positions. While your PSAP may not have the ability for the employees to reach all these levels, identification of the levels and advertisement during hiring will appeal to those searching for a career.

Mentor positions. These positions can start early in a public safety telecommunicator's career. Once the employees have a good handle of the job, new employees below them will welcome a friendly face to bounce off their concerns. Someone who can guide

8

them with positive feedback, encourage them to continue, and give hints on how they made it. Mentors can be someone fresh off their first year or entering their 25th year—anywhere within their career. A positive mentor is a helpful part of an organization. The only word of caution is one year on the job does not make anyone a pro – so use caution when giving job skills advice. The leadership team identifies mentors in the PSAP, or they may mentor naturally. Chosen mentors are best when they demonstrate positive behavior and good character.

Communications Training Officer or CTO. These positions are considered in many organizations as a first level supervisor. This is because a trainer's primary responsibility is to provide thorough training of another person. The CTO is the point of reference, the rule reminder and enforcer. Agencies lean strongly on their CTO program because the person the CTO is training will be sitting next to them someday as a partner. Mention this opportunity to applicants!

Supervisors and Lead Dispatchers. A lead dispatcher is not a level used by all organizations. The duties of this position, like that of a supervisor, vary significantly per PSAP. There is a saying that if you have seen one PSAP you have seen one PSAP. This is true in most aspects of the 9-1-1 environment. A lead dispatcher or supervisor may be referred to as a working supervisor. This means that the position has some supervisory duties but still needs to work in the dispatch position. The duties of a working supervisor will vary from direct employee oversight with commendation and corrective action authority, scheduling, and projects to watching over the working staff and helping. Other supervisor positions are tasked with oversight of the center, but not considered part of staffing. Projects are assigned to supervisors in this category to provide oversight, research innovative technologies for the PSAP, or function in an administrative/operations type position. Supervisors will often be in line for careful consideration and grooming within a succession planning process. Progressive responsibilities beyond their assigned task such as receiving new project assignments and having the authority to delegate aspects of tasks and projects to others can aid promotional consideration for those interested in succession planning.

Deputy Director/Operations Manager. This position may be one or two people. They are considered to be the "right hand" of the director or head position of the PSAP. Agencies may have a sworn person in this position, others have moved to a civilian executive. This position is responsible for the vision and direction of the organization. The position, when correctly filled, sets the culture, develops budgets, manages projects, and offers continual support for succession planning. Not all agencies have this level. I started my career with a law enforcement agency whose philosophy was to grow the skills of those who wanted "more" but did not have this level in the PSAP. The agency prided themselves on the rate employees were recruited to become chiefs and directors with other agencies after serving years at the agency. For some, this philosophy is tough to maintain when your staff leaves to go to other agencies. A shift in thinking can help every leader provide the best opportunities for the staff, understanding that after several years of service, their success and experience may lead them to higher-level positions elsewhere. For some agencies, it is not an easy pill to swallow to expend resources training someone only to have them depart to another agency, but with a vision shift, it can be something to be proud of. Your leadership and organization prepared them through years of training and experience for their growth and success. While the person was with you, their increased knowledge and developing leadership was a benefit to your organization. The leadership from your PSAP was their catalyst.

Other PSAP Related Positions. There are other positions within a PSAP environment that may be available to telecommunicators, and they may discover they are more suited to these positions. Information Services (IS or could be referred to as IT/Information Technology) is an essential position for the PSAP. Having the right people in place to protect the critical infrastructure is not for the weak-willed individual. This position requires knowledge about cybersecurity, NG9-1-1, and new technology and have the same passion to make a difference as a public servant as those who wear the headset and drive the vehicles! Telecommunicators making the switch to Information Services is a common practice finding them succeeding, growing their careers.

Working closely within Information Services is the position that works with the geographic information systems (GIS) for the agencies. This position manages all types of data for mapping, calls for service, crime mapping, as well as staying current with the needs of NG9-1-1 and the other public safety agencies served by the PSAP. It depends on the agency for this position, but some of the minimum requirements may be a bachelor's degree, experience with GIS technologies, familiarity with Computer Aided Dispatch (CAD) and Records Management Systems (RMS), as well as computer hardware and software experience and being self-motivated.

Then there are the opportunities for more advanced positions at a state or national level. Positions that include state 9-1-1 Administrators, National 9-1-1 Administrators, Chairperson or President of organizations. The 9-1-1 profession will allow you to go as far as you want to—it just takes commitment and vision. Perhaps if you are at the beginning of your career, you don't see it yet, but once a seed is planted, it has an opportunity to grow. The key is, there are growth opportunities everywhere you go.

If your position is to recruit and hire telecommunicators, it is your job to sell this profession as a career, not a seat to fill or a J.O.B. Helping applicants see the variety of possibilities they have has potential to increase your applicant pool in both quantity and quality.

Job Duties Preparation

As a new telecommunicator, career goals may include the opportunities we have listed here but learning the new skills must take precedence.

Recognizing 9-1-1 professionals' job duties does not have to be daunting, however it often is. In speaking to seasoned 9-1-1 professionals when they first started their journey in the career, they will reflect on those early days with statements such as these:

- Overwhelming
- Exciting
- Exhausting
- So many screens
- Tough to remember all the right questions
- Hard to adjust to different trainers
- Hard to adjust to different shifts
- Great feeling when you have helped someone
- WHY can't I get this!?

Answering the phones, talking on the radio, data entry into the computer, knowing geography, multi-tasking and switch-tasking are essential for successfully mastering the job duties. Preparing the candidate takes time, but pre-training the trainee could save you time and dollars later in the process. More on this later.

Benefits

Education

You have completed the first part of highlighting the career itself, although people may not stay for the benefits alone, remember the example supplied earlier that the benefits may be the motivation to look for the job in the first place. While not all PSAPs can offer advanced education reimbursement, this is a powerful incentive. Educational reimbursements can include a "pay-back" schedule if the employee leaves after graduation before an agreed-on length of stay. When I earned a bachelor's degree, my employer's reimbursement plan paid for a high percentage of the tuition. As part of the reimbursement agreement, I agreed to stay for four years, so they could see a return on their investment. When I earned a master's degree, the return-on-investment length of employment stay was five years. Each plan clearly outlined what my payback would be if I left earlier than the outlined terms. For example, a five-year plan could entail repayment of tuition at the rate of 90% if within the first year of completion, 70% if within two years, 50% if within three years, 30% if within four years, and 10% if within the fifth year.

Savings

Agencies throughout the country no longer offer full retirement benefits with full pension and medical. Recommendations for retirement contributions are 10% of gross salary for a start (The Investopedia Team, 2021). Retirement accounts are often in the form of 401K plans and a vesting period with a company match plan. The employer contributes "x," and the employee contributes "x." The employer typically contributes more than the employee, although the plans that allow for added employee contributions are an incentive. If the employee has a choice, the closer to a full 20% between the two, the better for the future. For plans that do not have the ability for additional employee contributions, agencies may offer a payroll deduction plan such as a 457. Offering an added 1 to 2 percent employer contribution may be appealing for applicants considering career opportunities between two agencies. This area is a good place to highlight when recruiting by showing the employee what he/she may contribute as a future savings plan.

Wage Compensation

This could be the icing on the cake for your agency or "good enough" so that your applicants are inspired to apply. Either way, displaying wages is a choice you must make. There is a current trend to not include wage/salary information in job listings in the private sector. As a public servant employer, wages are open to the public and cannot give an employer as much (if any) negotiating power with a new employee (Vyvial, 2020). Withholding the information in the private sector may be done because employers want to avoid competition between current and new employees or between other companies within the industry. Within the public sector, however, wages are often on a set scale and withholding them from an advertisement does not have the same effect. Wage comparisons should be completed every two to three years. If your agency is a union employer, bargaining for wage increases can look great for new applicants. New to public safety qualified applicants can currently choose any agency they are interested in because the need is so great. While this will not always be the case, making sure your wage compensation is comparable to others in terms of your service size, call volume size, and the expectation of your staff is important. Make sure your agency is comparable to or even above the average center with wages, other benefits, or both.

Recognition

Each agency has a unique-to-them recognition program. If your agency doesn't have anything, creating one is important for the culture and morale of the staff, given that research from Workforce Institute indicates that 82% of employees say they're not being recognized enough (Tremmaglia & Harvey, 2022). The arrival of the Great Resignation is suggested to impact 85 million roles (across all industries) to be unfilled by 2030 costing the global economy more than $8.5 trillion (Wilson, 2022). This alone should make it more important than ever to attract and retain the best talent possible. Creating a hybrid program using peer-to-peer recognition, inner-office games with rewards, regular evaluations, along with formal recognition can help create a more satisfied staff and cohesive atmosphere in your PSAP. Highlighting the recognition programs during recruitment is an added attraction to your PSAP!

Healthcare

Healthcare expenses are rising. According to the US Centers for Medicare & Medicaid Services, in 2021 healthcare costs rose 2.7% from 2020 to $4.3 trillion. Listed below, PeopleKeep provides eight reasons for rising healthcare costs, none of which PSAPs or public safety agencies have any control over.

1. Medical providers are paid for quantity, not quality. This results in redundant testing and overtreatment.

2. The U.S. population is growing unhealthy. In the 1980's, I recall the release of a prediction for mine and subsequent generations. The prediction stated that we would be the first generation in history to regress in longevity. Heart disease, high blood pressure, diabetes, and other chronic diseases have increased with the current statistic being more than half of the U.S. having at least one of these health challenges, driving up health insurance costs. The Kaiser Family Foundation shows an increase between 2011 and 2021 that on average premiums for family coverage rose from $15,073 to $22,221, an increase of 47.4% in just 10 years.

3. Technology is great, but for healthcare, the newer the tech, the more expensive the visit and tests.

4. Americans do not choose their own healthcare. When employers offer low deductibles or small office co-pays, it

can encourage overuse of the healthcare system, driving up demand and cost.

5. Healthcare is often bought without a clear understanding and knowledge of what is being offered.

6. Healthcare systems, through mergers and partnerships, can increase their prices in concentrated markets.

7. The fear of a malpractice lawsuit often causes doctors to overtest or treat out of fear of a lawsuit. This is referred to as "defensive medicine" and the average price of this fear-driven practice is around $100 to $180 billion annually.

8. Inflation affects the costs of operations, supplies, administration, and facilities. As patients increasingly return to in-person doctor visits following the pandemic, healthcare inflation is slowly increasing.

What does this mean to you as a member of the public safety community? Having the ability to offer more than one plan, and taking the time to explain the plans fully, will help your staff feel involved and able to make informed decisions when choosing a healthcare plan. If management is not able to provide clear explanations of the plans, the insurance company or the agency's insurance broker will be able to provide information. Offering low deductibles but having a portion of the premiums paid by the employee may seem like an answer to the agency's financial concerns. However, offering a low deductible and a high deductible plan will give employees options. Companies, both private and public, offer lower cost high-deductible plans and contribute to the employee's Health Savings Account (HSA). If employees understand how the cost of premiums, deductibles, and employer contributions to an HSA can be of benefit, it may lower the agency's expenditures while lessening the contributing factors to rising healthcare costs.

Insurance Opt-Out Incentives

For employees who can obtain healthcare from other sources such as a spouse or parent, offering an opt-out incentive can be greatly beneficial for an agency. This is true regardless of whether the agency is insured through a company or self-insured. As an example, according to the nonprofit organization that focuses on national health issues, Kaiser Family Foundation (KFF) website, in 2021 the average annual cost for single coverage was $7,739 and family coverage was $22,221. If the employee already has access to insurance (proof is required), offering an opt-out incentive for single employees of $2,000 and family opt-out incentive of $5000 (25%) will save the agency 75% of their healthcare costs for that employee. In addition, that's extra money for the employee, which is appreciated and viewed as a benefit!

There are a variety of reasons why people may choose public safety as a career. Your job as leaders in this industry is to show them why they would want to start a career and why they will want to stay! With honesty, transparency, and a path of continued growth, applicants will see this J-O-B as a career they can work in throughout their lifetime.

CHAPTER 2

Hiring Techniques

In the 80's (that's the 1980's!), part of the hiring process consisted of an interview, a check of your criminal and driving record, and a polygraph. I recall having the straps secured around my torso, a blood-pressure cuff around my arm, and my finger in a pulse reader and the multiple questions they asked. Some of the questions shocked my 19-year-old self. Do people really do that? Yes, I discovered later, people really do steal vehicles to make it to a job interview at the police department and use illegal recreational drugs so they can be relaxed while interviewing, information that poked holes in my rose-colored bubble.

Sworn personnel were also required to go through a psychological exam and a physical but there was little thought that the dispatch or records support personnel would need such an extensive background check. Through the progression of time, many things in the hiring process remain consistent and some have changed. In 1988, a legal ban was placed on private employers using a polygraph, also called lie detector test, for hiring. Federal employers, law enforcement and probation officers were not covered in the Act (United States Department of Labor, 1988) and many continue to use them. The agency I worked for stopped using them after the ban went into place as did other agencies in that area (and perhaps across the country because there was research released showing that a polygraph was not always a reliable indicator of a person being dishonest (Stromberg, 2014). Although the actual processes of background checks for new applicants have not changed significantly, there are portions of it that are more in depth because the realization that telecommunicators have access to confidential information increased the need to fully research their integrity.

Preparing Current Staff

When you're looking to begin a project (and recruiting, hiring, and training your first, first responders IS a project!), you first need to identify your goal, that is, begin with the end in mind. When a PSAP is short staffed, the current staff initially will fall into one of two categories.

The first category contains telecommunicators who are really excited about the empty seats because that represents overtime. Forced overtime is seldom utilized because employees love the extra work. According to David Bishop with SmartCapitalMind, the most common reason for employees to work overtime is labor shortages, which represent an opportunity to earn more income as well as a loss of free time (Bishop, 2022). There is also the Striver Syndrome which compels employees to want to look good in the eyes of supervision (Kelly, 2020). Often competitive people by nature, these individuals believe that soaking up the overtime will help them to look better than their peers who must be forced to work and may benefit them in the form of a promotion down the line. The challenge then is to recognize that although your agency may have a plethora of people clambering over the offered overtime, it is often associated with burnout, stress, and other mental illness. Research also emphasizes that those who work more than 10 hours a day are 60% more likely to have heart problems and higher blood pressure. The second category contains telecommunicators who are tired of working overtime – whether forced or voluntary – and they want relief.

At this point, you may think, "Why does this matter?" There are times when employers leave openings for the purpose of preserving the budget, space savings is the common term used when describing this delay in hiring. While overtime may be welcomed for a time, it doesn't take long, as all leaders know, for the staff to begin to experience burnout. Once hired, training will take four to six months before the new hire is considered part of staffing. Up until that time, shortages will be filled through overtime or perhaps even worse, shifts are left below minimum industry standards. Leaders know that the perceived benefit of space savings does not outweigh the benefit of filling the spot as soon as possible. Prepare the staff for the process, providing the organization with regular updates and a projected hire date for the candidates creates a two-fold benefit. It includes them by disseminating information to all and gives them an idea of what to expect.

Aside from a hiring update, pre-plan to select your trainers and determine the projected schedule for the duration of the training. Meet with the trainer and mentor team to ensure that all staff are aware of your expectations and have an idea of where the trainee(s) will go. Part of the expectation setting with your training unit is to go over the flexibility needed in a training program due to phases or sections of the program that may last longer or be shortened depending on the trainee. Once the trainers have met (easily accomplished with a virtual meeting), convey the information regarding the hiring status to all employees and provide regular updates as information changes. Current staff must not be told about the results of a background investigation other than if the applicant passed.

Recruiting

Accomplish the recruiting goals as frequently as needed or you can recruit once and establish a list for "x" amount of time. An important thing to remember is if you wait until you have an opening before you begin your process, the burnout from overtime and frustration from current staff is going to intensify. Life happens for employees—they experience marriages, births, divorces, deaths, educational pursuits, or an offer for a different position or career that they cannot pass up. There are usually a few who are actively looking for greener pastures. While you can anticipate these events, you cannot always predict their timing. In the example of the birth of a child, the employee may insist that she will return after the baby is born only to discover that she isn't able to leave her new child and submit resignation papers only days before her scheduled return. Beginning a process *before* there are openings will speed up the time from vacancy to a floor-ready employee. We discuss the variety of methods for recruiting more in Chapter 5.

Remember to reach out to your public safety agencies as well as your staff for referrals. The family, friends, or acquaintances of your current staff may be a good fit in your 9-1-1 center. Consider offering an incentive to your staff for successful referrals. Offering an incentive after the referred person starts work or upon the completion of training is a good motivator. As a reminder, if your staff recommends family members, make sure you review your current policies and/or bargaining contracts regarding relatives working together.

One PSAP in Colorado hired a public relations firm to create a recruitment video. They budgeted about $8,000 to have their 9-1-1 dispatch center highlighted with all the wonderful things you get as a dispatcher in a PSAP that has all the finest equipment, staffing, camaraderie, promotional opportunities and in the great state of Colorado. They highlighted the community, surrounding parks, and a wide array of activities for your family. It was intended to attract not only local dispatch candidates, but also candidates who might be interested in relocating their entire family to the area. It was very inspiring and almost had me convinced to move!

An underutilized location for finding applicants is from local high schools. Asking school administrators for a time to talk to the seniors or provide brochures is a great way to "start them young." Several years ago, the agency I worked with received a request from a local boy to see if he could volunteer in our PSAP. We did not have a volunteer program at the time, but we had him come in when he could, and he would have observation time on the floor. At the time this started, his mom had to give her consent and drive him to us because he was not old enough to drive. During his visits he expressed a desire to accompany the dispatchers to public speaking events and hand out coloring pages to children. He enjoyed doing that and it sparked a creative side to him we were not previously aware of. After a brief conversation about the products we had for handouts, he sent some items he had designed to help. Full customized books with 9-1-1 information and wonderful drawings. He continued that until he was well into high school and then off to college. We didn't hear much from him for a while, but later we discovered he was working in an area 9-1-1 PSAP. Although we were disappointed he was not working at our PSAP, it was exciting just the same to see that his interest as a public safety telecommunicator had stayed intact for all those years. A volunteer program is a great way to find future full-time telecommunicators. It is especially fulfilling to offer it to high school and college students as an intern position. Allowing time each visit for observations (because sitting with the dispatchers is the cool part), volunteers can assist in a variety of tasks including organizing resources, typing documents, and reviewing policies (to make sure they are understandable for someone with no public safety knowledge).

Vocational schools have public safety/criminal justice tracts for high school juniors and seniors. In Ohio, my co-worker Karen collaborated with the instructor to implement and maintain a 9-1-1 certificate program. It was a 2-year program for juniors and seniors and each year, she would go to a school and speak to the junior class about how to gain employment as a telecommunicator. They would discuss background and education, on the job training, interviewing, pay and benefits and potential to grow or move to another field of public safety. In their junior year, they started with a textbook and simulator training for call taking and radio communication. In their senior year, they would visit the PSAP and observe the dispatchers in action as a group field trip. In the following weeks, the PSAP would allow two students at a time into dispatch for an up-close sitting "under the headset" with their dispatchers. Normally they had five dispatchers on shift. By limiting the number of students to a four-hour block of time, this ensured that the student got the best experience by having a variety of individual dispatchers who would share their headset experience. The students then had an assignment to write about the experience. Karen said it was enlightening to her, as the manager, and to the dispatchers who showed them the real-life dispatch experience. Overall, it was a great program. In 2020 they paused any visitors in the PSAP due to the pandemic.

This starting point for entering dispatch has many benefits. As a young person getting out into the world, you don't know what you don't know. For a candidate who is studying public safety and wanting to get into the field, it is a great start—a win-win for the employer and the employee. If they are planning to continue onto college studies, working part-time as a dispatcher is a great way to learn more and gain experience. It is also a great way to help pay for college and potentially keep the employee full-time for a long career as a dispatcher.

I had several positive experiences with hiring a part-time pool of talent as they were beginning their career. Jeff was fresh out of high school and starting his first year of college. He wanted to become a firefighter and paramedic. While attending college, he worked as a dispatcher and the knowledge and experience he gained provided additional insight into fire and medical emergencies. Once he completed his degree work, he continued to dispatch for about 4 years. He moved on to the fire service and today is the fire chief of a city with 30,000 residents. Another part-time dispatcher, Sara, was attending college and decided to go to law school. She graduated and passed the bar and continues to work full-time as a dispatcher. Her student loan is offset because she is working for the government, and the dispatch center benefits from her great knowledge of the law. Like I said, win-win.

Having a pool of part-time telecommunicators complements your full-time staff if you can add them and, as I said earlier, it saved my career. Depending on how it's established, your commitment may be limited because it is part-time, but they can fill in for you on short notice or a set number of hours each week. I see it as contributing to the overall public safety experience for employees and employers alike. However, this may take some work on your part. If your agency has never had part-timers, they may hesitate to entertain the idea. Believe me, it is worth the investment. I have had part-timers who were:

- Full-time dispatchers from other PSAP's
- Former dispatchers who wanted reduced hours after leaving in good standing
- Administrative assistant for police chief
- Former police officer on disability retirement
- Husband/wife, son/daughter of fire or police officer

You need to respect the fact that you are only offering part-time. That means you must respect the other commitments that are making them want only part-time hours. Be respectful to them as a person and an employee, and the culture will build itself. I was able to add them to our collective bargaining agreement. This was important to show they deserve some benefits. For example, if they worked on a premium holiday, they received extra pay for that (i.e., Thanksgiving, Christmas, New Year's). After all, they didn't need to volunteer to work so a full-timer could use vacation for those events. If I was going to have to pay overtime to cover that holiday shift, giving a part-timer some respect and a bump in pay would be cost effective and reasonable to expect them to work. Full-time holiday pay for example could be time and a half plus. Part-time holiday pay could be straight time plus a set amount extra per hour as a premium. It is much less than the full-time wage, yet acknowledgement to the part-timer that they are valued in the organization.

Part-time staff will also appreciate the ability to earn benefit time. Providing part-time employees with the same opportunity to earn benefit time off, at a part-time rate, is appreciated because when vacation time comes up, the part-timers can take time off with pay. Although this benefit was not used by the majority of the agencies near mine, I experienced great success with our part-time employees' benefit time.

Your full-time staff may not like having part-timers. They may try to take advantage of them. They may talk down to them. Or they may be grateful to them because they take away some of the overwhelming overtime. Either way, if you have a union, it is important for union shop agencies to get them in the bargaining unit with specific language of how the part-time role functions (how overtime is covered, minimum/maximum hours per week, benefits, etc.). Management can protect against some of the bullying that may arise, especially when mandating overtime shifts for short notice call offs or vacations. Having part-timers who already work in public safety to some extent can lessen the training curve to get them fully on board.

If your PSAP only has full-time positions, it is essential that you staff appropriately for the workload. At any time, a full-timer may experience an unexpected injury or illness. When this happens, it is almost impossible to stay within the budgeted line-item for overtime. I have experienced the loss of full-timers for up to 4 or 6 months and covering that only with overtime from the other full-time staff does two things. First, it blows up the cost of wages and second, it burns out those who are working overtime. This is a bad combination for the organization and difficult to get ahead of. With your hiring needs keep this in mind and make sure you know your backup plans should you lose a few full-timers unexpectedly.

Education and Testing for Applicants

When our son Matthew was 19, he informed us after his first semester of college that he was going to join the Marines because he was tired of everyone telling him what to do. His recruiter had told him of the financial and career benefits he would be experiencing in the military as an Air Traffic Controller (ATC). Our son proudly told us that once he signed up and completed boot-camp, he would be making more money than we did. We smiled (knowingly) and gave him our full support to serve our country as a U.S. Marine. Keeping this funny, but true story in mind, make sure you educate your applicants with an accurate picture of their future in public safety!

Perhaps years ago, the need to educate applicants for a career in 9-1-1 was unnecessary. As the saying goes, times have changed! Today's workforce wants to know what they are getting into. The good, the bad, the ugly, the money, the benefits, the time off—they want it all BEFORE they accept the job offer. How then do you begin an education program before they even step through the door? Each PSAP has a choice of possibilities. For the next steps, you could buy a program (Equature offers a great product, World Class Online Interactive Learning for 9-1-1 Dispatcher Training), you could design your own, or you could research your state's guidelines. Regardless of the decision, at its core, educating applicants before they start will save your agency time and money.

The education process doesn't have to be complicated, but any educational process followed by testing does need to be "vetted."

You may have heard that term before—it means to make a careful and critical examination of something. In this case, having a process that is vetted will ensure that it's been reviewed by others, that there is an established baseline for testing purposes, and that it meets civil service requirements, even if the agency does not fall under civil service standards. Having a process that meets the criteria is good defense against any accusations of wrongful hiring practices. For a career in 9-1-1, these tests include mental ability and skills required for the position in accordance with the job description. It also allows for physical testing validation to meet the standards of hearing, vision, and drug usage screening.

What better way to screen applicants than to provide them with a thorough training of what the job entails and then test them on what they learned along with basic mental and skills abilities that coincide with the job descriptions. Using the established baseline for "passing" the exam, the applicants moving forward are better equipped to understand their duties and responsibilities in a 9-1-1 career.

Another education piece to embed somewhere in the process prior to a job offer is a two- to four-hour observation period on the dispatch floor. If this is clearly outlined as part of the testing process, you can require applicants to schedule a time for this within the process. Before the observation time, make sure the applicants are prepared by asking them to compile a list of questions they may have. Equally important is preparing your staff with a similar list of things to cover and require documented feedback of their time with the applicant. While a CTO is usually a good choice, an employee whose goal is to become a CTO is a valuable option. It allows the employee to experience a quasi-training environment and it allows supervision to see how well the employee does.

For the rest of the story regarding our son, as it turns out, he did need someone to tell him what to do and in fact thrived in that environment. He has served our country for over thirteen years and is at the current rank of Gunnery Sergeant. He plans to retire after 20 years, as a Master Sergeant ATC and to this day, he laughs at his 19-year-old self as much as we do.

Interview Process

The interview process can be wherever in the sequence that best fits your agency. It can occur first to quickly reduce the list of applicants or at the end after testing has been completed. Putting it after an education and testing process provides management with basic knowledge of the applicant's abilities. The interview process will then assist confirming that information. You find people can test well yet interview poorly and visa-versa. Your interview process helps you zero in and ask pointed questions, perhaps even from the education session, to gain knowledge of the applicant's aptitude.

Depending on the number of applicants you have, once the orientation and testing is complete, you may consider setting up a quick 15-minute phone interview to see if your offer is what they are looking for in the job. They should understand what the job is and is not, at this point. They may have additional questions about the agency, who you are and why you are hiring. Ask for a little history and then set up the in-person interview or tell them you will contact them for the next steps.

Some agencies will pause in the process at this point and do a preliminary background check with a couple of phone calls. You already have their application and past employment. If they have indicated that it's okay to contact current employers, do so or call the previous employers! Often applicants do not want their current employer to know because of fear of retaliation if the employer finds out the applicant is looking for new employment. Violating that request in the beginning can result in the loss of a good candidate. At some point, the current employer should be contacted but do this with the applicant's knowledge. When you are in leadership for any amount of time, you will experience the frustration of finding out that one of your employees was hired at a neighboring PSAP and no one called for a reference check. As long as you have a thorough section that has been signed for a release to do a background check, this step will save you time and money by doing this ahead of the in-person interview.

If available, have a greeter on the day(s) of the interview. This person can change if the process is longer than one day as a consistent review of the applicants will not include this person. The greeter will meet each applicant, check, and copy their driver's license, provide them with any paperwork they may need (code of conduct or ethics documents are good to get into applicant's hands at this point). The greeter can also provide schedule reminders to assist in keeping the process flowing. The person can facilitate any typing test and a review of the original application to verify any changes that may have occurred. While there are many configurations of an interview process, one that has been tested and effective is one that includes current staff and public safety customers and or partners in a two-step interview process. This can tie up a lot of resources during the day(s) of the interviews because the interview panels must be consistent throughout the process (same people for the entire process). Having the interviews run in unison will help move the process along. A two-panel interview process includes a group of three to four current staff members. CTOs or future CTOs are best because it gives them strong buy-in for their future peers. A panel of supervision, public safety customer(s), and even a future supervisor is a great mix for the supervisor panel. As much as possible, the manager/director (whoever is making the final hiring decision) should stay out of this process, allowing it to work as designed so that the top position can do a final interview later.

The two panels running back-to-back interviews should meet between each person. For example, when the peer panel is done, before the applicant moves to the supervisor panel, any concerns they notice should be addressed. There are other tasks the applicants can do during this process, some agencies require a minimum typing skill, others may just want to see how the applicant maneuvers a keyboard. If you have a word-per-minute (wpm) typing requirement, make sure you run a test for it. If the applicant has poor typing skills, this could be an area to focus on during the interview and training if the person is hired. Not meeting the minimum wpm doesn't have to disqualify an applicant if the decision to move applicants who cannot meet the standard is applied consistently for all. There are several free typing tests online that not only give you words per minute in real time, but the candidate can also practice improving to your standards. Years ago, it was not critical. Today, accuracy with a keyboard is essential.

How do you prepare your interview panels? If you have an HR department, contact them prior to the interview process and go over what you can and cannot ask during the interview. For example, questions about age, national origin, children, disabilities, faith, and sexual orientation are not allowed. Your job description and posting should clearly identify the requirements regarding disability. For example, hearing and vision must be able to be correctable within normal ranges as an essential function. Do you then disqualify those who are color impaired? Not necessarily. I worked with a person who could only see shades of gray and was a very good dispatcher. Your baseline testing will identify areas of concern, so it should not enter this initial interview process. Before the interviews, have the panel members arrive early enough to go over the details of the process as well as make sure everyone is informed of any follow-up questions that may violate the applicant's civil rights. Make sure the same primary questions are asked to every person. Understanding that depending on the answers, different follow up questions arise. Also, if the interview is really tanking, don't waste your time or the applicant's! One applicant once told the hiring board that she had smoked marijuana two weeks prior because she felt pressured at a concert (using any drug substance may be considered a violation depending on how your policies are worded. For example, drug usage may be acceptable if it occurred "x" years ago.) You can end the interview when an applicant becomes disqualified. You're in charge of this process and interviews are not a guarantee for applicants!

The same baseline questions must be asked for every applicant, with the same standards used for scoring, preferably by the same interview panel. Here are some examples:

Why have you chosen this field?

0-1 Does not show a great depth of knowledge for the field.

2-3 Shows some understanding of the field.

4-5 Was able to provide solid examples and understanding of the field.

What is your most significant weakness?

0-1 Does not have self-awareness of any weakness.

2-3 Indicates a weakness that is contrary for this work.

4-5 Shows full awareness of weakness with action plan for correction.

What have you done to prepare yourself for this interview?

0-1 Does not indicate any extra tasks taken.

2-3 Indicates some review of the profession.

4-5 Indicates review of the profession and organization, possibly some observation time at a 9-1-1 center.

When preparing your questions, make sure you know why you are choosing the questions. Remember you are testing for skill, so use the interview process to gauge character qualities and find out more as to how the applicant prepares, thinks, reacts, and functions in life. Your standards reflect what you are trying to determine with each question. The spread can be wider, which would allow for greater subjectivity in the panel. This type of subjectivity is limited within the defined standards. Make sure there is a space for notes and encourage the panel to leave their thoughts regarding the score they provided or an answer that really stuck out. Remind them however that these documents are part of a retained legal file.

The numbered standards should be given with the end in mind, meaning what is the highest score possible? For ease of scoring, pick a top score such as 25, 50, 75, 100. Have enough questions to take thirty to forty-five minutes for an interview, giving the panel fifteen minutes before the next applicant to score, discuss, and stretch before the next applicant arrives. When discussing the applicant, and this is important, make sure the discussions are not used to change anyone's score. The process should be solid, and the scores should stand on their own. If panel members influence each other for scoring purposes, then the purpose of holding a multi-member panel is futile.

Make sure one person is assigned as the "in-charge" person for the process. This person will make sure everything is in order and running smoothly and on time. The assigned person is also responsible for providing the final summary of the process for however many of the top applicants that have been decided on. If you need to hire five, consider sending seven qualified candidates to do background checks.

Background Check

Background checks are performed throughout the hiring process. Screening applicants for driving status, warrants, and criminal history before they start the process is acceptable if the application has a clear release of information statement that the applicant must sign and date. Doing a quick screen before starting the applicants in the process may thin out the application pool, but it is better to discover early on that your applicant has a warrant or unacceptable criminal history. A few years ago during the orientation process, there were applicants who showed up with active warrants. Our local law enforcement agency was present to advise them they were not eligible to continue in the process and that they needed to take care of the warrant. Although no one was ever arrested at the event, there were several over the years who were turned away and advised that they needed to take care of their history.

Trained personnel should conduct a thorough background. This may be a supervisor in the organization, local law enforcement, or a hired background investigator. 9-1-1 personnel have access to the same information as law enforcement and NCIC and state systems require that individuals who have access to the information contained in their system meet the requirements. Background checks, at a minimum, should include:

- Local records/contact request from agencies where the applicant has lived and worked.

- Checking with former employers regarding the applicant's on-the-job performance.

- A review of documents provided by the applicant which can include school transcripts and credit reports as well as other pertinent information that may be required by your agency.

- A neighborhood check, speaking with the applicant's neighbors regarding their actions or activities in the neighborhood.

- Calling all references.

- Asking the references for other names (not on the reference list) that may be contacted. This will allow the background investigator to speak to people NOT on the reference list and sometimes provide a different picture of the applicant. This picture may be a green flag (hire quickly!) or a red flag (danger, danger!).

- An NCIC and local computer check to make sure nothing has changed since the beginning of the process.

When all the information has been collected, a report for each section is typed and provided to the hiring manager/director for review and decision on the next step.

In addition, consider psychological assessments to evaluate the candidates' mental state and thought processes. In my last PSAP, a well-established firm was retained to do our assessments. The firm specialized in public safety and the agency was able to customize an assessment for our specific hiring needs. We gave them several traits and advantageous characteristics of what makes a great dispatcher. From there they created a specialized 150 question assessment and would analyze the results. A full summary was then reported back to us with potential areas of strength and weakness. This firm did pre-hire screening as well as employee and executive assessments for our entire organization.

After this portion of the process, the final decision maker(s) should have a final interview set up with the applicant. Reviewing all available information, make the questions for each applicant similar while still flexible enough to address any concerns found during the process. When this portion of the process is complete and the applicant has passed all steps, consider a baseline hearing/vision and drug screening as well as a psychological examination. You may inform the applicant that you are giving them a conditional job offer pending the outcome of these final steps. These final pieces to the hiring process will cost the agency (covered in Chapter 5). It is said that it is better to do a psychological screening BEFORE the applicant is hired than to do a Fit-For-Duty examination after hiring the applicant. Realizing two or three years after employment begins that the struggling individual never should have received an offer does not help you or the organization. People can often cover up their inner personality for a time, but when it reveals itself to you, believe it! Make sure you have a highly regarded and recommended doctor and facility for the psychological testing. You want the information clearly provided to you in a written report so that you can understand their final hiring recommendation.

Final Offer

At last, the final offer can be made. The process is long and sometimes drawn out over several weeks. Arriving at this point as efficiently as possible is beneficial to the organization and the candidates. Too long of a wait time from application to final offer can cost you some amazing applicants when they accept job offers from other agencies.

Provide the candidate with a phone call of the final job offer before you send an official offer letter. I have personally experienced this phone call ending with the applicant refusing the offer because they've decided dispatching isn't for them. Very frustrating but regardless of how much you educate and work with the applicant, it still happens. Count yourself lucky that you found out *before* you spent more agency dollars and time training someone who most likely would not have worked out.

When you make that final offer, have the start date and schedule for at least the next six weeks set. Provide them with their pay rate and any wait time they may have for insurance activation. Provide all the information to them verbally with a follow-up letter sent (email is fine as long as the document is a pdf.). If the letter is sent digitally, make sure you ask for a receipt and applicant acknowledgement that the letter was received. Provide the letter to the training supervisor and trainers so that everyone is informed of the same information.

Onboarding

The onboarding process can make all the difference when it comes to a new employee's experience and set them up for success that will surpass the training and probation period. Onboarding at its core is the process by which new employees are initiated into the organization. Following the steps listed in this chapter are part of onboarding. Consistent communication on the next steps with the applicant, education on what to expect, and meeting staff during the process are all part of the onboarding experience. Successful onboarding provides key information to the applicant/new employee regarding their place in the organization, policies, culture, and processes.

When the new employee starts officially, have them meet with a designated person to fill out appropriate paperwork. If the paperwork is sent to the employee ahead of time, this will speed up this tedious process. The paperwork includes W2's, payroll information, HR documents, employee handbook, bargaining contract receipt, whatever paperwork that can be sent and printed and returned by the employee on the first day will help make this process easier. Have emails and computer logins completed and printed on a document to give the employee. Most PSAPs have a variety of logins (phones, internet, email, apps, state systems, etc.). Each of these should have the employee preloaded so that passwords can be assigned. Helpful onboarding also includes reviewing the policies and expectations of the employee before they start with the designated trainer. If your agency is hiring more than one employee at a time, consider accomplishing this as a group in a mini-academy or classroom setting. Providing the trainees with an overview of the computer systems and how to sign on and fill out basic information for a call for service will help your trainers focus on the details of the job from day one.

If you have uniforms, getting the employee's sizes prior to the start date will also make sure that they are provided with the basics on the first day. Some agencies have a wait time before uniforms are issued, if this is the case, consider purchasing at least two polo type shirts with your agency logo so that they will feel part of the team from day one.

This onboarding experience will go over the training schedule, the trainer's approach, and the process for training both in and out of the center.

Let the trainees know how often they will have check-in and coaching sessions in addition to the regular training they will receive. Let the employee(s) know when there are mandatory meetings they will need to attend. You can organize all this information in an inexpensive pocket folder and even include a small piece of candy as a welcome gift. It gives the trainee something to hold on to and gives them a good feeling about the upcoming training and the agency in general.

Onboarding, technically, can last as long as the first full year but the intense part is in the early days of employment. Your goal is to get to the point where the employee is a productive team member. Provide some easy-win tasks to give the employee a sense of accomplishment early on and throughout the process. Understanding that the job is not for everyone and no matter how many easy-win tasks you provide, the basic skills of the job must be met.

The final step in onboarding is to ask the new employee for feedback. Provide them with a document that is easy to complete. Have them provide feedback from the start of the process to hiring.

When the training is complete consider having a mini-interview process to examine their experience with the organization, trainers, supervisors, and peers. Encourage honest responses and ensure that their remarks remain confidential.

CHAPTER 3

Training for Success

Training for success, is your first thought, well duh - why would we train for anything less? Hopefully, it will be something along those lines! Years ago, I was introduced to the phrase from a neighboring agency when I was told, "We can't keep the newbies because our trainers (or their peers) eat our young." This is a terrible analogy, but one that is prevalent throughout the industry. At one agency I went to, the trainer came up to me and proudly proclaimed that it had taken him less than one shift for his trainee to quit. The phrase according to the Idioms Free Dictionary means to neglect, betray, or harshly criticize members of a group that are of lower status or position. The example is exacerbated when the more experienced staff treat trainees and new employees with sometimes intolerable contempt, thus accused of "eating their young."

Eating their young is another way of saying hazing in today's terms. Hazing, as a verb, has one definition in the Merriam-Webster dictionary that means to attack repeatedly with mean put-downs or insults. Hazing can have significant consequences and liabilities in today's workplace.

Think about this—your agency has invested time, effort, and money into the hiring process to produce the absolute best candidate for the position. Having no patience or tolerance for questions or errors and making sure the person knows it, is a way of eating the young. If an intervention does not take place, eventually the new employee will fold under the pressure and leave, producing yet another opening. Why then, can this behavior be allowed? "Well, we don't like her/him, or she/he annoys us," are examples of statements I heard frequently from the would-be-peers regarding the trainee or newly released from training probationary employee. The trainees and newer employees will absolutely make mistakes and feel unsure in situations for up to two years. They will have different personalities and mannerisms. Some truly cannot perform basic functions of the job and must be released. Others may become so insecure in their own abilities after a barrage of criticism, cold-shoulder behavior, and whispering gossip mongering, that they begin making multiple mistakes and cannot stop the spiral. These are the people that need rescuing.

I think many PSAPs have that one senior dispatcher, like Sally, who takes pleasure in making the trainee feel inadequate. Sally could have the most seniority and her family is filled with police and fire officers. She knows it all, in her eyes. As a CTO, she is known for making the trainees cry. All the staff knows about her and has witnessed or experienced her behavior. It is a joke with the veterans, but it is all too disturbing for the director or manager who must ensure that onboarding is done in a more professional manner. Sally is quick to say a trainee is not going to make it. Within the PSAP, her exceptional knowledge of dispatching and how to find information within the computer systems is crucial when training new hires. Counter that are the harsh criticism and words of discouragement toward the trainees – which is not what is wanted in a PSAP culture! Ultimately making her a poor choice as a CTO.

Some of the best shifts I have ever worked are with those who get along, they celebrate each other's special occasions, and create a warm welcoming feeling for anyone who steps onto the dispatch floor, regardless of rank or shift. They also worked exceptionally well as a team, during crises and tasks they remained professional and productive. This culture throughout the organization is a plausible goal, although it is possible to be productive without that camaraderie (it just is not as fun of a workplace). Leaders of an organization have a duty to insist and enforce professionalism through training, encouragement, and recognition for jobs well done. It is the only way to help employees of every level understand their role in the training process. Dashe & Thomson is a company that addresses specific business goals and needs. They reported that lack of management support and lack of executive involvement are in the top three reasons why training programs fail (Lueck, 2017). From the lowest seniority person to the highest, the success or failure of a trainee can hinge on current staff.

The trainee's experience not only includes your telecommunicators, but the other agencies' employees you interact with as well. When you have the dispatcher do ride time with your fire department, make sure you have an outline of topics that you want them to discuss. Examples include types of vehicles, why the typical response has a certain number of personnel or apparatus, high hazard businesses and other agencies with specific topics. Having training officers fully engaged in seeing the success of the organization is crucial.

Where is your dispatch center located? Is it within the police department or is it in a separate facility with a separate employer? This can influence how the police/fire officers perceive the dispatchers. With a consolidated dispatch center isolated from other public safety response agencies, there can be agencies who want to see you fail. Change is a difficult concept for people to accept. If you are the leader who decided to make a drastic change, there will be lasting hard feelings. This is true because there are so many personalities that make up our safety forces. Be aware of this and make sure you deal with it head on. Your trainee will quickly recognize a disgruntled police officer who is gruff or rude on the radio or phone. Avoid having that officer do the ride along with your trainee! Beware of those who want to sabotage your efforts because they do not like the changes that their dispatchers have made.

Do not misunderstand this information because there are legitimate circumstances when the trainees simply cannot perform the job functions. Despite the best efforts to get the highest quality candidate in the door, this career is not for everyone!

Generally speaking, "three strikes and you're out!" Teaching is an art. Your CTOs will all have their strengths and weaknesses. If it is not working with one, change to someone else. Personality, tone of voice, personal bias, what is happening at home—these all play a part in the training experience. If after you have taken all this into consideration and the trainee still is not progressing in the program, make the cut. Your trainee may just thank you for it.

Consistency

As a start, to achieve consistency in training, all involved in training should attend the same training-the-trainer training, or Communications Training Officer certification class. Ensuring that your CTOs are professionally trained is critical for liability purposes. Using the knowledge and skills gained in the training program, develop a training manual to keep each trainer following the same path in the program. The training manual should include all the training, expectations of the trainee, expectations of the trainer, and a clear understanding of how the weeks of training will unfold.

Consistency, however, will require more than a manual for each person to follow. Every new person in training will experience different challenges, successes, and roadblocks on their learning path. Bringing the trainers together for a meeting every four to six weeks while there are trainees in the program will provide each CTO with an overview of the trainee's progress while currently in the program. It will also assist the designated trainer if there are areas where input from others would be helpful. During these meetings, the CTO supervisor and/or director can provide training tips and instill character building for the trainers. Reminding the trainers to not discuss trainee's progress (or lack of) with non-trainers will help keep the trainee's from being dismissed, which in the Oxford language dictionary means to treat an unworthy of serious consideration. Keep the meetings to sixty minutes with the time used constructively. Virtual or in-person meetings work equally well. There are advantages and disadvantages to both venues. Knowing the staff's challenges for meetings and remaining flexible to benefit the majority will help the meetings to be more productive.

CTO/Trainee Meetings

CTOs are with their trainees every workday. They are imparting their knowledge to their protege with each incoming call, each radio transmission, and each item listed in the training manual. There may be questions then as to why they would need a specific meeting on a regular basis. While interviewing trainees in regard to their completion or failure to complete the training program, the complaint that they did not have sufficient opportunities to meet with the trainer and training supervisor was frequent. Ensuring a requisite number of the trainer review meetings by senior leadership is imperative.

Trainees and their CTO should meet regularly depending on the schedule. No more than three workdays should go by without a detailed shift meeting of where the trainee is in the program, areas of concern (if any), areas to work on (constructively presented), and remember to always highlight the areas they are achieving their goals. These meetings should allow for the trainees to provide feedback on their status as well. Documenting the meetings, by both the CTO and trainee, is a must (I know, more paperwork!). A Daily Observation Report (DOR) is a common tool used to document the trainee's progress, or failure to progress. The DOR examples are often supplied in the CTO class. Creating your own with your agency specific requirements is encouraged because no PSAP is the same. In the Appendix are two samples of DORs presented in Equature's CTO class, taught by Tony Harrison. This documentation allows both to put in areas they feel comfortable and areas requiring more attention. If there is a significant incident during a shift, and a meeting not possible until the next day, the CTO should make sure the trainee knows they will have a brief meeting at the end of the shift or if staffing allows, have a quick debriefing meeting immediately to go over the incident. A significant incident could include a high priority incident or an incident that the trainee managed ineffectively causing delays or an inappropriate responder response. A significant incident could also be a priority call that the trainee performed in a stellar manner. Going over it with them as soon as possible really boosts their confidence, which is very beneficial to new hires (everyone actually—it always feels good when we have done a good job and made a positive impact). Remember to document everything—the good, the great, the ugly!

Trainees, CTOs, and the training supervisor should also meet regularly. I recommend it once per week. This next level meeting will include only the current CTO, but the documentation will be available for all CTOs. In this meeting, like the CTO/trainee meeting, the trainee's current status, successes and areas for improvement are covered. The CTO supervisor can also take this opportunity to check on how the trainee is doing with the trainer and other staff, after excusing the trainer from the meeting. This portion of the meeting needs completion only in the middle and end of each training phase unless there are apparent concerns.

Flexibility

How flexible should an agency be for the benefit of the trainee, agency, and program? The answer is not simple. As the saying goes, back-in-the-day, agencies took a hard pass on flexibility. Candidates were plentiful and usually, "no," was the short answer then. In current times a long answer is more appropriate and complicated. Agencies can determine how flexible they will/can be with a new employee's previously planned events. Ideally the conversation regarding planned events or conflicts should start before the new employee's first day, as early as the interview after making a conditional job offer. A simple question, "Are there any planned vacations, events, or other things that you would need time off during your first year?" If there are, remember that your newest employee had a life before the job offer. Paid for vacations, weddings, and special event tickets will be important to the employee. Flexibility, to a point, is helpful because it can assist in reducing the stress of the newbie. Note the term, flexibility to a point. The agency can either deny the leave time or grant it, letting the employee know they would need to use benefit time (if they have any) or go unpaid. While going unpaid may not be ideal for the candidate, the flexibility shown by the agency when approving time off for their planned event will go a long way. Keep in mind, you still must follow any bargaining contract regarding time off without pay (non-disciplinary) as well as any policies written on the topic. It is also important to make sure the employee is focused on successfully completing the training program. New employees need to realize that excessive time off will hinder progress, creating delays in having the employee as a contributing team member.

FMLA employers and employees must meet federal guidelines to qualify for this protection within the law and workplace. Employees who may need time off during their probationary period may not qualify under the Family and Medical Leave Act. Check with your law directors or human resources for exact guidance, but here is the condensed version:

- First, the trainee must have worked for the employer for at least 12 months.

- Second, the trainee must have worked 1250 hours in those 12 months, or about 24 hours per week.

- Third, the employer must have 50 employees within a 75-mile radius of your worksite.

Twelve months and 1250 work hours is not realistic for a new hire to have. However, if the employer…you…wants to attract and keep trainees in your program, you should accommodate, if feasible, when the need is there. If you have a trainee who is expecting a baby in three months, you can get a good chunk of training done in that time, allow them to be off for the baby, then start up when they are ready to return to your training program. Do not lose good candidates by staying inside the box. Think outside of the box to solve the individual trainee's problem. In addition, the law states that the employer must have 50 employees within a 75-mile radius. That does not mean the employer who has less than that cannot follow the FMLA laws. Make sure your policies reflect the culture you want to develop. The FMLA law states the minimums, your policies can develop from there to reflect more leniency or strict adherence to the law as written.

Vacations are one type of planned event, keep in mind a planned event may be, "oh, by the way, I'm expecting a baby in x months." Or "while I was waiting to hear if I would be hired, I joined a military reserve unit." Having experienced both, there is a frustration that may occur at the leadership level with this new knowledge. You are the professional. Smile and roll with it anyway! Childbirth leave (including adoption) is allowed for up to 12 weeks' time off using FMLA time. Employees on FMLA must remain on payroll, including benefits. For employees who pay for benefits, if they are going unpaid, make sure the method for continuing payment for benefit coverage is pre-arranged. For military leave, how the agency compensates the military employee can be flexible, no pay or benefits, benefits, supplementing time (this occurs when the employer makes up the difference between the military pay and the agency pay), or full pay. However, the law prohibits employers from denying military time regardless of whether the employee's service is voluntary or involuntary. It is also unlawful to withdraw your offer of employment for these types of reasons. Clearly communicating to all involved, how the upcoming event will impact the training program is required, keeping in mind that any medical reason, including pregnancy, cannot be discussed with any of the staff unless written approval is given. To do otherwise is a violation of the Health Insurance Portability and Accountability Act, referred to as HIPAA (U.S. Department of Labor, 1993).

If an employee has already started and notifies supervision of a planned event during the training period, providing the same flexibility is just as important with the new member as it was before his/her first day.

Failing Forward

Training programs should be set up to review trainees for the areas they are struggling in. In a numbering system, they may spend a full week getting ones. Without the proper framework in place, the trainee can really struggle with constant reviews of "ones." John Maxwell is a leadership expert, speaker, and author. He wrote about Failing Forward in all aspects of life. There are several of his principles for failing forward that can apply to the training atmosphere. For trainees to fail forward they must understand that they are going to fail. Exposing trainees to these concepts during their first days in orientation will assist in setting them up in a failing forward concept. Seeing failure as a temporary problem, while accepting the responsibility for their errors is part of the principle (Maxwell, 2011). The CTO should help the trainee set and understand realistic expectations. Having unrealistic goals dooms them to failure. Help them understand that setbacks are normal and that everyone fails in the beginning!

As the training continues, CTOs must help the trainees focus on their strengths. Maxwell stated that people operating from a position of strength enjoy a far lower rate of failure than those wallowing in the areas of weakness. This does not mean the weak areas should be ignored. Providing the trainees with different approaches will help them bounce back. Anyone who trains knows that a bad day can really set progress back. Encourage trainees to learn from their failures, realize they can't go back and do it over, but they can move forward and do it right. Maxwell stated that he believes it is nearly impossible for any person to believe he or she is a failure and move forward at the same time.

There are a variety of programs available to help track progress. The key is they must be measurable with specific standards in place and what the employee is doing to be at the level given as well as how they can succeed.

If one does not exist, have your trained CTO team develop Daily Observation Reports (DOR). Given that you would want to have them all attend the same train-the-trainer course will provide you with the framework. This form should provide quantitative measurements of the performance in each category and written observation of performance for the day. The goal is to provide feedback that is measurable to the trainee that tells them what they need to improve, are competent in, and what they have mastered; then reviewed and signed by the CTO and the trainee. This will also give the director or manager an overview of the progress. There are programs available that have the entire process digitized. This is an excellent way to decrease the paperwork for the CTO and make the information available to the training team.

Examples of the quantitative portion of the daily report include things like appearance, attitude, use of radio, customer service, tone of voice, knowledge of policy, prioritization of call types, and listening skills. Develop a rating scale something like this one:

Rating scale for DOR

Unacceptable   Acceptable   Superior

1   2   3   4   5   6   7   8

This is for your agency, so you decide what scale makes the most sense for your success. Scales can contain any given range of numbers. The key is to have an unacceptable, acceptable, and superior range.

When recording a daily written log of the trainee's activities, highlight the strengths of the day by providing a detailed description of the strengths. It does not have to be long; it can be as simple as:

> *Today trainee Smith used excellent tone and control when answering questions for an incoming caller. Trainee Smith continues to demonstrate compassion with the callers regardless of their emotional state when they call.*

This narrative will help your trainee to continue to "fail forward" by using descriptive words and a clear picture of what occurred. This type of review may take an extra fifteen seconds, but the review provides a more concise overview than one that says, "Trainee Smith did a good job on phones today."

Identification of Deficiencies

Address deficiencies in the PSAP quickly. Educating the trainee on what they did wrong but coupling it with how they can improve or do it differently. Better still is to have the trainee tell you how they could improve. Modern day employees desire an opportunity to explain why they did what they did—they want their thought processes heard. A CTO could view this as an argumentative behavior, but there is a better way. Taking it as an opportunity to see how the trainee thinks is useful in helping them achieve their training goals. Recall that they have already been set up to accept responsibility for their actions but that does not mean they will. The job of the training program is to make sure they are feeling and experiencing success while still learning and improving the number of deficiencies.

Document deficiencies right along with the strengths. Make sure the trainee is part of the process by documenting his/her own struggles using a thorough description of the event. As shown in the examples of failing forward, teach the trainee to document struggles like this example:

> *Today, I took several calls and did not verify the address with the caller. My CTO explained why this is so important and how addresses can be incorrectly given by the callers. It makes more sense to me now and I will correct this in the future.*

As opposed to this type of documentation that does not provide a description of what occurred:

> *Today I did bad verifying addresses. I'll do better tomorrow.*

The CTO should be descriptive of errors and accept nothing less than descriptive statements from the trainee. Actually, typing or writing this out will help the trainee realize the error and could help improve his/her performance quicker.

Remedial Plans

Once you have tried all the tips for immediate improvement of the trainee with little forward improvement, it is time to consider a focused remedial plan. Explaining this pause in forward training to the trainee should come as no surprise to him/her, but they might find it hard to accept. Communication with the trainee is crucial. People who are in a remedial situation may begin making more mistakes because they are so nervous. Explain to the trainee to be careful not to put needless pressure on themselves. Help them to understand that this is not a punishment, rather than an opportunity to have a do-over to master crucial skills. Even providing a non-public safety reference may help. Informal golfers will take a "mulligan," otherwise known as a "do-over" when they hit an errant shot. This is an opportunity to have a do-over in areas that the trainee is struggling in (Harvey, 2010). Keep in mind that there are sometimes trainees who will not succeed in the PSAP. Also remember the time, effort, and money invested into the trainee, and this is an attempt to help the trainee prevail. There are different definitions of remedial training. The one that fits this scenario comes from *definition.com* and it states, "This training is offered to overcome the deficiencies or shortcomings in the performance and behavior of the employee." Creating a remedial plan for improvement is achievable with trainees because it gives them full buy-in for the process. Remedial plans can also be prepared and presented, but the status of the trainee should never come as a surprise to him/her. The daily interaction and specific meetings should provide a clear overview of the progress. If remedial action is necessary, the trainee should be expecting it based on the daily exchange. It may look bleak, but I have personally witnessed and been part of trainees put into remedial training who have emerged as successful, long-term employees.

Make sure the employees and the training team know that you are extending a remedial training program, often referred to as a Performance Improvement Plan. Remedial plans should have one to four specific areas that need improvement. The plan should include what the deficiency is, exact expectations, detailed steps of what will occur during the remedial time, and time frames to reach the goals set out along the way. Time frames vary but should be sufficient for improvement to take place. Two work weeks to six is a common period. When a trainee is in remedial training, all additional training should stop, meaning putting on hold adding new skills to their knowledge base. This does not mean that the trainer should not take advantage of discussing an opportunity that presents itself during the daily tasks. It just means that intentionally covering new training material will pause.

CTO programs cover remedial training often providing how to set up the plan for the trainees' best success. Clearly, however, a properly set up plan also provides solid documentation of the steps taken to help the employee in the event of termination. Negligent retention is a significant agency liability, as are negligent hiring, supervision, and training. Negligent retention occurs when an employer fails to take appropriate steps (training, discipline, termination) against an employee that the employer knew or should have known was unsuitable or not performing and the employee's actions cause harm to others. An individual can file a liability suit against the agency for negligent retention if these elements are in place. Liability in these cases lay with the agency as well as the management who knew, or should have known, of the negligent events.

Shadow/Check Out

Shadow, the final phase in a training program where the trainee is functioning as a full member of the team with the trainer "shadowing" him/her. The trainee is to rely on his/her own training and experience, asking the team members questions if needed. The trainer acts only as an observer, documenting the process carefully. The Oxford Dictionary provides the definition of shadowing as "follow and observe (someone) closely and secretly." This phase of the training is NOT done in secret and the trainee must know exactly what is expected. Agencies will have a pre-shadow built into the last phase of training. A pre-shadow is like a shadow with the exception that the trainee can still seek out the trainer for questions and guidance. When a trainee is successful in the pre-shadow, it sets them up for success in the check-out phase.

Trainees with Prior Experience

You see the potential when the applications come across your desk, PSAP or public safety experience. In all the years of being in leadership, this has always been a welcome application, full of potential. Potential to bring in someone with different views and/or to shorten the training time and get some relief for your current staff. Prior experience can be, as they say, a blessing and a curse. Properly vetting this application is important because adding a problem employee to your staff will not solve anything.

Prior experience can shorten the training process, especially depending on where the applicant is from and may offer cost-savings as well. (See more on this in Chapter 5.) An agency that has any of your current systems will reduce the needed time spent on that subject. The applicant may have experience with the same 9-1-1 phone system, or CAD. Experience can also help with state systems and NCIC. They may have advanced protocol training, they may already have classes in place to meet minimum training requirements, and they may have habits you will need to break. Experienced dispatchers can really struggle in a new agency, particularly if they have been with their current or immediate prior agency for any length of time. I recall hiring an employee from a neighboring agency within our county—law, fire, EMS, state and NCIC system experience—this person had it all. The only task would be to train to our standards. Two months into the training, I was giving pep talks because it proved much harder than the new employee expected. It is helpful to have a standardized document called a Performance Improvement Plan (PIP) ready if needed (sample included in Appendix). A PIP is known as an action plan, a tool to give an employee with performance deficiencies the opportunity to succeed. The plan identifies, at most, two or three specific areas. It clearly conveys what is not at an acceptable level and what actions are needed to improve. The PIP must be measurable and have an end time attached. There were moments when the employee nearly resigned, but we developed a focused PIP to cover the areas of weakness and the trainers were able to pull the employee out of the slump and released a confident asset to the organization. But it did not end up being a significantly shortened training process—every trainee is going to be different. They will bring their own learning styles, strengths, and weaknesses. The goal of the training program is to discover the learning styles, strengths, and weaknesses, and work within those parameters.

Failing forward is an important aspect throughout the entire training program, all the way to the final check-out. It does not stop when the trainee is released from training. All team members must be willing to assist if the new employee stumbles. Assist, not take over unless there is a genuine problem that the new employee cannot handle. It is at this point that the culture of the team must be in check. Providing a helpful atmosphere from the employee with the longest longevity to the newest—the tone of the center must exude a strong team front.

How many trainees can your PSAP handle at once?

It is important to engage your existing staff with the planning aspect of onboarding. You want to be fair to your CTOs and keep the safety of your officers in mind. Training takes the CTO away from dispatching in the normal fashion. They will be more focused on the trainee and the specific topic at hand. This makes it a bit unfair to expect the CTO to fill in a regular dispatch position on the floor. This number will depend upon the size of your agency. You also need to make sure that the dispatchers who are not with a trainee understand that they will have to help pick up phone and radio traffic that they might not otherwise. Safety to the officers and the public, and fairness to the existing staff will dictate the number that is right for your PSAP.

Technology to Help Train

Technology is ever changing. I daresay that by the time this book is published, technology will offer something newer that won't make it into these pages. Even so, here is a short list of some of the tools that can be useful in training:

- Transcription Tools sit with the recorder software (offered by Equature). This A.I. powered transcription engine transcribes live audio and video in real time. It can be copied and pasted into other documents (such as CAD or a word document) for a trainee to follow along and listen during a QA process.

- Video 9-1-1 calls can help the trainee use visual tools to guide the callers through directions and provide descriptions of scenes. This tool, for some products like Connect, will also provide a mapping tool that will show the dispatcher/call taker where the caller is on a map. In addition to the live video stream, seeing the caller's location on a map can help orient the trainee to locations in the jurisdiction.

- Virtual assistant tools, driven by A.I., can provide trainees with a place to go to search and ask questions. These A.I. processes are growing in popularity not only as an extra tool to have in training, but also as a go-to search engine specifically designed for public safety. The chatbot EVA (Equature Virtual Assistant) as an example is designed to provide feedback, guidance, and suggestions for handling emergency calls as well as identifying potential areas for improvement. With automated quality assurance and quality improvement features on the horizon in A.I. 's future, tools like EVA will continue to become smarter. The information and assistance that is provided will grow in sophistication and can easily be incorporated into training programs and everyday environments.

Exit Interview

The CTOs have tried all the tools available to them. They have documented every move the trainee has made and all efforts point to a dismissal. Releasing someone from employment is typically not a pleasant experience but for the good of the agency and of the person, it is sometimes necessary.

Prepare standardized questions that can be used for all exit interviews. As a brief example:

1. What did you enjoy most about your employment here?
2. What changes would be beneficial?
3. How was the communication with your leadership?
    a. Supervisor
    b. Deputy Director
    c. Director

For exit interviews with trainees who did not complete the training program, add information specific to the training program and the CTO. These questions can include things such as:

1. Did you have regular and specific meetings away from the council regarding your progress with your CTO?
    a. With your training supervisor?

2. What did you find beneficial about the training program structure?

3. What do you think would have been a helpful change in the training program structure?

When conducting an exit interview, begin with your end goal in mind:

- How are your trainers doing?

- How is the training process going?

Remember throughout the interview that your interviewee may not be in a productive mood (angry, sad, argumentative, etc.). Do your best to get past the emotional words that may be used and hear what is being said that may be useful. Even angry employees can often offer information that can bring about positive changes.

CHAPTER 4

Release from Training

Released from training, all the weeks and months culminate with this final event for the training program and finally filling the empty seat in the PSAP. But is it really the final step for the training program? The easy answer is no, the long answer is it depends on what you consider your training program to be. As of this writing, there are national recommendations for emergency dispatcher training, but there are no federal mandates. Forty-three states have training requirements matching the national recommendations set forth by NENA, APCO, and 911.gov, an extensive training recommendation document named the Recommended Minimum Training Guidelines for the Telecommunicator. Each topic has a sub-category associated with it that provides in-depth topics.

➢ Legal Concepts

➢ Roles and Responsibilities

➢ Interpersonal Communications

➢ Emergency Communications Technology

➢ Call Processing

➢ Emergency Management

➢ Radio Communications

➢ Stress Management

➢ Quality Assurance

➢ On-The-Job Training

The training program is just the beginning of career-long training. Lailah Gifty Akita stated that "Every beginner possesses a great potential to be an expert in his or her chosen field." A true statement for any profession, but in the PSAP, we strive to create a room full of experts. It just takes time and the proper processes in place.

Review of the Training Program

In modern days, the rules we follow (policies, procedures, and protocols) are either recorded on paper with ink or produced in digital form and often stored in a digital format within the security of the organization. The point? The rules are not written in stone. Stone carvings have been around since the Stone Age when prehistoric people created petroglyphs to communicate and record events. It was not until 105 AD that the Chinese created a paper substance to record information. We are far beyond that now and utilize easily reviewed digital products, adjusted on a regular basis according to changing laws and the needs of the PSAP.

One effective way to review the training program is to ask the newly released trainee about his/her experience in the program. One training program calls this process the Board of Evaluators (BOE), and it provides a safe, confidential place for the trainee to provide feedback on what they liked, did not like, or thought should change as well as providing feedback on their trainers and training supervisor. Gathering this information has helped mold a stronger, more efficient training program while addressing areas for improvement needed within the CTO group. The BOE produces a written review and can detail the plans for change within the document. The plans for change can prove important because often, in the busy atmosphere we function in, our ideas get lost or forgotten completely. Said so many times before, document, document, document – and this holds true for this review as well.

The BOE can consist of the top members of the leadership team but does not include peers of the CTOs and the training supervisor. Do not share any remarks regarding a performance issue with peers. Having said this, it is common for the training supervisor to be present and excused when it is time to ask questions about the training leadership. The questions should be, as they are in an oral interview, pre-scripted and relevant to the information you are seeking to learn about. Examples of these questions are:

- What part of the training program did you find most helpful?

- What part of the training program did you struggle with?

- During your training, were there any tools that helped you, either those made available to you or things you developed to assist yourself?

- Did your CTO adjust to your needs as a trainee? Please describe specific examples.

- How often did you have one-on-one meetings with your CTO?

- Throughout the training program, was there ever anything that surprised you?

You can also use this part of the process to answer any questions the trainee may have on benefits and scheduling. Asking the question, "do you have any questions regarding your schedule" may not be sufficient. Remember, we don't know what we don't know. It is hard to answer that if you don't really know what to ask. The trainee may believe he/she understands all the processes, until you start with a high-level overview.

Excuse the CTO Supervisor

- How often did you have meetings with your CTO supervisor?

- Was your CTO supervisor or shift supervisor easily accessible to you?

As with an oral job interview, the answers may spark back-up questions so make sure you ask your follow-up questions. In addition, the newly released trainee may need reassurance that the answers are confidential. You could also prepare a brief survey for the trainees and ask them to complete it prior to your BOE. Focus the questions on how to improve the program and look at the organization through the eyes of a new employee. It is possible to discover that the atmosphere and culture you thought you had is not at all what it seemed. It could ideally be better, but it could also be a disappointment that leadership will need to address.

Schedule this meeting as soon as possible once the trainee completes training. This is not a conditional offer meeting; it is an opportunity to gather and disperse information. At the conclusion of the meeting, prepare a letter to the newly released trainee going over expectations and reaffirming the topics regarding benefits, schedules, etc. Do not put any of the BOE answers into this letter. It is just an information and congratulations letter.

Continuing Education

Providing continuing education for employees is a critical part of leadership's responsibility. Not offering or providing continual education throughout the tenure of the employee leads to liability issues. Two of the best examples are the topic of stress management and technology. Stress management is not a one-and-done training. People experience stress for varied reasons, personal lives, financial, and work. Provided training should also attack the causes of stress. The best way to do that is to determine what the employees perceive as the root causes of their stress before sending them off to a stress management class. For example, beyond an initial stress management class, training provided to help employees do their jobs better can be an important way to reduce stress (Tyler, 2021). Nearly one-third of calls in a PSAP produced peritraumatic distress which a study by the Journal of Traumatic stress linked to 9-1-1 dispatchers experiencing post-traumatic stress (PTS). Employees who feel more confident on how to process calls for suicidal callers, domestic violence, child callers, active assailant, as examples, can reduce the effects. More on this in Chapter 6.

Technology is changing the way PSAPs do business and will continue to evolve. Providing training regularly regarding new technologies already in use and those being considered may help reduce anxiety about technology the employees have heard about but have received limited information. Consider this: The Bureau of Labor Statistics indicates that jobs for public safety (law, fire, EMS, 9-1-1) will continue to grow by an estimated 8% through 2026.

Work in a PSAP is not static, and neither should your employees' skill levels be. While there is training that needs repeating, ask your staff, tenured and new, the type in which they are interested. If it meets the criteria of improvement, either specifically work related or self-improvement that can benefit them on the job, send them as often as you can. They may only get one class per year due to budget and staffing constraints but helping them help themselves will go a long way in retention and morale.

Oversight of Progress

Even experienced leaders can sometimes fall into the trap of making assumptions about their employees' needs. When a trainee finishes their training period, it's easy to get overwhelmed with other priorities and neglect proper follow-up. Many managers have found themselves in this situation before—assuming the newly released employee will seek out help if they require it, while the manager focuses on the twenty other tasks on their desk. The most effective leaders realize when this happens, they course-correct, and make an effort to check in with and support newer team members, despite their busy schedules. They understand the importance of providing guidance during the transition period from training to independent work. With some self-awareness and adjustments, any manager can avoid these oversight pitfalls. By being aware, you will not find yourself in what feels like a sudden development, discovering that the employee is faltering, and requiring additional training. I have talked to dispatchers all over the US and Canada and it has always amazed me the number of dispatchers that only have a vague idea of who their director/manager is. Truly, I have been so busy that I often went home at the end of the day realizing I did not eat and barely remember restroom breaks. While I was always successful in seeing all the dispatchers, I also recognized that the leader of any organization may be amazing, but by not rewarding the staff that does the work, in this case the dispatchers, the organization may be unsuccessful.

Strong leadership and oversight, not to be confused with micromanagement, is a fundamental building block for accountability. The Information Commissioner's Office stated that the highest senior management level or decision makers must lead by example to prompt a positive culture[23]. Showing your new (and experienced) staff that you value them can go a long way for the organization, cultivating higher morale and ensuring that all members of the PSAP know the expectations. Being present does not mean you are looking over everything people do, second guessing and interfering with the leadership team's decisions, and taking over tasks from the employees. Micromanagement often occurs because of lack of leadership skills and trust in the staff. Another contributing factor is the fear of losing power and position. Good leadership will make suggestions and discuss ways to improve rather than give orders. Top leaders and decision makers can be active in their PSAP by making sure the system around them is functioning properly. Doing spot checks, asking questions, and trusting your team will help keep you from being surprised when a new employee is struggling. Remember, like everything we do, setting clear expectations will help people function in a cohesive culture.

Remedial & Recognition

In Chapter 3, we discussed remedial training as it pertains to the trainee. Specifically, we discussed tools used to pause their development, assist in reinforcing employee achievement, detail areas of concern without punitive intent, and focus on their growth so that they can then continue on with their development. For the first year of employment in the PSAP, employees may struggle in areas that were not apparent in training. Or they may start feeling relaxed in the work atmosphere and begin displaying undesirable character traits. Whatever the challenge, remedial training may occur at a variety of points in the employee's learning path. When an employee is struggling, the first step involves talking to the employee to find out what is occurring for them. They just completed an in-depth training program so making sure a conversation takes place is important. They may have had a personal challenge to deal with and a quick reminder of the critical nature of the job and an offer of the Employee Assistance Program (EAP) may help get them back on track. On occasion, remedial efforts are put in place only to find out that the cause of the employee's indecisiveness and errors occurring while dispatching are related to supervision in the workplace. Employees require guidance while performing theory tasks, especially newly recruited persons. When faced with complex decisions employees need help from supervisors, and peers, and encouragement on how to complete the skills properly. Without supervision, employees rely on their own skill sets that may result in delays in dispatch, officer safety issues, and an excess amount of other liabilities. Make check-in conversations with the leadership (all levels, supervisor to CTO) on-going. The remedial efforts described in Chapter 3 have been known to get employees back on the right track.

I cannot understate the importance of recognition at all levels. As a director, I often left the recognition of the line-level staff to the direct supervisors. This was a mistake. A dispatcher popped in my office to say "hi" one morning. She was just chatting about work when she looked at me and said something like, "You know, telling the dispatcher they did a good job and why on calls would go a long way." She went on to explain that the letters and their name on the Kudo board was nice, but having the director acknowledge a well-done call with a simple sentence or two, is meaningful. It was eye opening to me because I was always looking for ways to recognize the dispatchers for a job well done and passing that on to their supervisors. Getting the media involved was a struggle for our agency, being close to a large major city eclipsed the involvement of the media in our medium-sized center. When I was initially promoted to supervisor, my former peer, and yes, she was a friend as well, took me aside and told me two things I had to do and throughout my leadership career I did not forget the advice. Now that I was in supervision, she said, remember where I came from and always bring candy. There are a variety of recognition programs that have minimal impact on a budget. Employee of the month based on a strong quality assurance and improvement program can have rewards such as blue jean day (for centers with a uniform dress code), special parking, longer break time, and making sure the entire staff knows what actions achieved the recognition. The recognition programs can be more than leadership to staff, they can be peer-to-peer as well.

One of my other mistakes in recognition was not asking the employees what they might include as meaningful recognition. For several years, I hosted an annual awards ceremony which included a full meal for the staff and their families. Usually held in December, I provided games, cookie decorating, Santa, small presents for the kids, and a plethora of food. Yet, unless mandated, about half of the employees did not attend. In the last year of a planned banquet, I worked with the Union Leadership to pick the date that would work for them as well as determine activities and food. Planning went well and on the day of the event, one of the union members I worked with, along with the person's entire shift, would not even join us for the meal. Because of this, it was the last year for a banquet. These types of events were not the type of recognition that they found important. On a monthly basis, I provided candy, snacks, and ice cream nearly every month throughout the year, thanking them for the job they do and how critical they are only to have an employee tell me that while that was nice, it wasn't a necessity because they don't really "like" the recognition. Finally, I asked what the employees wanted, and they wanted a tree drawn on the wall so they could recognize each other. Taking this idea, I commissioned an artist to paint a giant tree on the wall for a peer-to-peer program where the employees could write out their praises on little birds or leaves and stick them on the tree. We maintained the Kudos board by putting incoming letters, emails, or recognition for specific incidents there. Lastly, but not least, I made an intentional effort to acknowledge excellent calls when I heard them or found them on the recorder while doing quality assurance. The employee that had stopped by my office came in one day and commented that everyone noticed the effort, and then she thanked me. Just a short thank you, but isn't it nice to hear no matter where we are in life?

CHAPTER 5

The Great Fallout

Telecommunications Shortages

In 1983, I interviewed for my first paying job in public safety. I drove half the night to get to the interview and I was tired, but I passed the first hurdle of the process! Following that was a background check and a polygraph examination. Soon the job offer came and I had my first "grown-up" job. As a new dispatcher, I recognized that if I did not make any mistakes, the job was secure. I started part-time, and it took six months for the first opening to be promoted to a full-time position. From there I remember that many people were hired behind me over the next few years. The tenured dispatchers stayed in place at the top, on days and afternoons. It took me four years to have enough seniority to bid off the midnight shift. That was in the 1980's, when I was being paid $7.14/hour (part-time call taker starting wages, a full-time dispatcher started at $12.00) the paycheck was like my golden ticket to independence, so much higher than the minimum wage of $3.35.

Shortages in public safety are not new. Throughout my 40-year career in the public safety field, there were few times when the PSAPs in the states where I worked, including my own, were fully staffed. As a director, I was fortunate enough to work at three different PSAPs where we maintained staffing between eighteen and twenty-four months with no turnover. During local, state, and national meetings I attended, public safety leaders would announce the number of vacant positions they had at their PSAPs, patrol, fire, and EMS. I was grateful during the times our vacancies were low, but I knew, and our leadership team knew that our time was coming, and it always did. The difference between 10 years ago and current times is more the number of valid applications that are received and the rate and reasons for the turnover.

An article released on September 5, 2021 by the Philadelphia Inquirer reported on a shortage so significant that 9-1-1 lines were ringing unanswered. The article continues by citing a decline in interest in jobs amid "calls for police reform and the national racial reckoning sparked by the death of George Floyd…" (Dean, 2021).

A study released by the Behavioral Insights Team and the University of California at Berkeley in 2020 reported that the level of 9-1-1 dispatcher burnout has increased, leaving vacancies across the country (Gilbert, 2019). The study showed that over 40 percent of 9-1-1 dispatchers exhibit elevated levels of burnout—the rate is more than double the burnout rate of employees in other fields. Add the high stress to the attrition rate and decreasing pool of applicants and shortages in public safety staffing abound!

Supplementing Telecommunications Shortages with Sworn Personnel

The migration of sworn dispatchers to civilian dispatchers began slowly and is still in process for many areas in the country. Listed below is an abbreviated list of reasons that agencies use to justify the use of sworn officers:

- Officers have a better idea of callers' needs.
- Officers can effectively screen calls.
- Dispatch is a good place to put injured or disabled officers.

- Officers can be called in from detective or patrol to cover a dispatch position.

Over the past two decades, the use of civilian personnel in the PSAP has become increasingly common. In many independent PSAP Authorities, the civilian telecommunicators are not allowed to screen calls for service which may tend to annoy responding officers. Specifically, hiring personnel whose career goal is to be a dispatcher provides more stability to the PSAP environment than those using the position as a steppingstone to other public safety venues. The training that telecommunicators go through often encompasses a comprehensive program of the basic duties, advanced technologies, as well as a ride-along program with law and fire (some may allow EMS ride-along as well). Agencies that send law and fire personnel into the dispatch center for observation time experience a stronger cohesive environment because there is a clearer understanding on both sides of the radio.

While patrol, corrections, or detective personnel may have worked in dispatch prior to their current profession, they may not meet on-going training requirements for work in the PSAP. With the significant technological updates which require training and consistent use, sworn personnel may not be up to standards and minimum training requirements required of PSAP personnel, just as PSAP personnel may not be able to meet the standards of law enforcement. Working in a PSAP requires its own set of skills completely different to sworn police officer powers and certification requirements. The Legal & Liability Risk Management Institute states that "Police agencies have an obligation to train their police officers for the recurring tasks that officers will face during their career. Where it is foreseeable that a police officer will face a particular task that may result in harm to another person, the officer's agency must provide training in how to conduct that task in a manner which is consistent with generally accepted practices in law enforcement". As the staffing crisis continues across the public safety profession, there is a reduced ability for agencies to train sworn personnel to do their expected tasks along with a telecommunicator's expected tasks. The report continues to highlight attacks on training (or lack thereof) over the past two decades have become one of the weapons for persons who file lawsuits against police agencies. In February 2022, Phoenix Police Department released a report that it had begun to use transitional duty employees (sworn personnel) into the Communications Bureau to assist with certain types of calls for service, thereby reducing the calls previously dispatched to patrol (Williams, 2022). This movement was meant to support communications and patrol by off-loading the dispatched calls for service.

Supplementing with sworn personnel may also have unanticipated results. Officers must attend a police academy so they can become law enforcement officers, not dispatchers. The technology in a dispatch center in the current environment requires on-going specific training for PSAP personnel that sworn officers often do not attend. There is also a pay discrepancy between the two professions and supplementing a civilian position with the higher paid sworn position can cause low morale, increased absenteeism, and even a pay classification dispute. 911.gov, NENA, APCO, and as of this writing, forty-three states have minimum training standards for their PSAP personnel. At the very least, best practices for 9-1-1 telecommunicators are completely different from the training and best practices of sworn personnel. Some states even have specific laws regarding the extenuating circumstances that must be met for a PSAP to supplement with sworn personnel. Chiefs, sheriffs, PSAP leaders, and PSAP authority boards have a responsibility to protect the organization. Simply stated, supplementing a civilian-staffed PSAP with sworn personnel is a liability disaster in the making and is best avoided.

As consolidated PSAP centers continue to evolve and expand to save money, eliminate excessive redundancies, and provide the communities with a more experienced staff, the ability to use sworn personnel to supplement continues to become an antiquated practice. Agencies operating under a Council of Government (COG), or other separate employers eliminate the ability to use sworn personnel to staff the communications center because the PSAP is a separate entity. It is not functioning as part of the law enforcement agency.

Cost of Hiring

When calculating the expenditures needed for hiring a new telecommunicator, keep the formula simple and thorough.

Advertising

Placing ads with organizations is a wonderful way to obtain wide national or international coverage for your opening as well as garner interest from locals who watch the job openings. Your state organization may or may not charge for the posting, the national organizations do have a fee.

Consider advertising (or just getting the word out that you are hiring) at the following locations:

The advantage of these websites is that they put your opening in for free or at low cost.

- Social media sites - LinkedIn, Facebook, Instagram, etc.
- Your public safety customer's website
- Your PSAP website
- Your Medical Control Authority
- State Communications organizations such as NENA and APCO
- Other state organizations you may have in your state (every state is unique)

- Local colleges with or without law/fire/EMS training programs

These next locations usually charge a fee. The advantage to these locations is that they reach an expanded audience. A word of caution, when using forums that reach a vast expanse of the public, make sure your process clearly details the qualifications (clear criminal history, background, no warrants, or drug usage as examples). This could save you the time and effort of going through hundreds of applications from people who are not qualified.

- Local or regional newspapers

- Billboards on local business or highways

- Local staffing agencies such as Mancan or Kelly Services

- Hiring websites such as Indeed, ZipRecruiter, CareerBuilder, LinkedIn

- National public safety websites such as NENA, APCO, IACP, EMS and fire organizations

Depending on where you advertise, advertising can be an expenditure of $0 to $300+.

Interview, Background, and Testing

Involving current staff in the hiring process is the best way to ensure you have buy-in from the ground level up. As discussed in Chapter 2, involving employees from the application process forward is an excellent way to start. Referrals are one of the most common ways to involve employees in the hiring process. Where better to find your next telecommunicator than from those already working and believe the person they referred to apply, would be a good fit? Providing incentives for them when their recommended person is hired and completed the training program is a nice benefit. Not only do they have a peer they have helped come onboard, but they also receive recognition. For my agencies, there was no room in the budget for hiring incentives such as this. When I first started offering incentives, I would get the employee who provided a successful recommendation a free meal gift card (enough for two) at a local restaurant. That became expensive since I was paying for it myself. Over the years I scaled back to a $5.00 to $10.00 gift card for ice cream, a specialty drink, or a convenience store snack. While not all the employees appreciated the scale back, most were still happy with a thank you card and the gift certificate.

Using the processes we reviewed in Chapter 2 (recruiting, education and testing applicants, interviewing, background checks), we can calculate each expense for the interviewing, background, and testing with actual employee expenses. Note, we do not include the leader, administrator, director of the PSAP in any of these calculations. Usually this is part of the regular job description and is part of doing business. The following table is an example of expenses and uses $25/hour for the PSAP employees except for the background check which uses $30. This is, in most cases, a low figure.

Orientation (2 employees) 3 hours @ $25/hour	$150
Testing (2 employees for proctoring, reviewing, preparing report) 3 hours @ $25/hour	$150
Peer Review Panel (3 employees) 8 hours @ $25/hour	$600
Oral Interview Panel (2 to 3 PSAP employees) 8 hours @ $25/hour	$600
Background Check (40 hours * $30)	$1,200
Drug/Hearing screening	$150
Physiological Testing	$400
TOTAL	$2,650

This figure does NOT include test development or purchases.

That brings the process to $3,050 - just to develop a hiring list of eligible applicants. Now you are ready to hire!

Training

The average on-the-job training program for PSAP personnel is five (5) months with programs varying in length of time. There are a variety of training topics for a new hire, both out of the office and in the office. When preparing a document for your superiors that shows the expense of hiring, each PSAP is different and has different programs. The National Emergency Number Association (NENA), the Association of Public-Safety Communications Officials (APCO) and 911.gov have developed best practices for training that include topics in these areas (not an all-inclusive list):

- Telecommunicator roles and responsibilities
- Stress management
- Liability/legal concepts
- Interpersonal communications
- Technology overviews
- Call processing
    - High risk
    - Hazmat
    - Homeland security
    - Law, Fire, EMS
    - Special needs
- Emergency management
- Radio communications
- Quality assurance

- On-the-job training guidelines

In addition, agencies using Emergency Medical Dispatch (EMD) must complete the required training prior to allowing the trainee to answer the phone solo. Many states have minimum training requirements that include these topics in a 40-hour basic communications course. On-the-job training will include all topics specific to your PSAP such as policy review, local laws/ordinances, geographic boundaries, and specific techniques.

Calculating expenditures for out of office training is simply adding up the full expense of the class and related expenses.

Training Expenses

Staffing shortages due to lack of new hires, also referred to as warm bodies, is a drain on existing staff when there seems to be no end in sight. Trainee after trainee, the CTOs have steady training duties and overtime. Being a CTO is hard in the sense that these dedicated individuals are training their *partners*—the people they want sitting next to them in a crisis. It is the CTO, as a quasi-first line supervisor, who is responsible for the errors and successes of the trainee and most times, they will go home at the end of each shift mentally exhausted. To calculate the CTO expense, using the incentive pay for the time spent training is a simple calculation. These are considerations to consider when revamping your training program and highlighting the expense of continual hiring practices.

Although whenever possible it is best to show actual figures, you may highlight overtime due to shortages under soft costs. A soft cost, a term frequently used in the construction industry, but the meaning is still the same for public safety, is an expense not considered a direct cost. In this case, the agency will have overtime costs due to staffing shortages. It is not a direct cost in the hiring process, but it is related.

The training expense for the trainee is an easy wage and benefit calculation. Your goal with this expenditure is to show why a hiring process and/or training program needs adjusting. Trainees are not considered part of staffing in most agencies because of the liability of having them work solo before a proper training program is completed. Using an average wage of a new hire as $20 for 6 months (24 weeks * 40 hours * $20) equates to $19,200 trainee expenses for wage compensation only. If the trainee is successful in the training program, this is an excellent investment. If the trainee is not able to perform the necessary job duties and is terminated after 3 months as an example, that still equates to $9,600 in wages plus the hiring process expense.

Also calculated in these expenses, if you highlight the amount the agency expends when the trainee fails to complete the training program or a probationary period, this figure often shows the need for and importance of hiring the best person for the position.

A Communications Training Officer (CTO) may receive an additional amount of wage incentive to be a trainer. Use this number to assist in calculating the CTO expense. In addition, you should calculate required overtime because the CTO is unable to do his/her normal duties because of training.

At this point you should have a good understanding of what the cost of a newbie telecommunicator is as well as the training, hiring, and screening process.

Mitigating Expenses

The simply stated solution to mitigating the expenses of hiring, is to put every tool in place to hire the right person for the job. When PSAP's are short staffed, there may be a tendency to hire a person who is not fully qualified, meaning that they did not score well on the test but interviewed nicely or they scored great on the test, but the interview went poorly. While sometimes people cannot manage the stress of taking a test and do poorly, consider that those who are poor test takers may struggle under the stress of taking the test. How then, will they do in the stressful environment of a PSAP?

A strong pre-employment screening process will assist in the reduction of bad hires. Employers lose more than 79% of negligent hiring cases, meaning they knew or should have known information about an employee's background that may have indicated dangerous or untrustworthy acts. Ensure that the applicant has solid credentials meeting the criteria set by the organization. To keep costs down, PSAP leaders may want to cut out parts of the interviewing process. This would be a mistake. Having a testing process that involves the current staff not only ensures that buy-in for the hired applicants can begin before the trainee steps in the door, but it also ensures that your applicant can successfully complete a test of basic duties or knowledge base.

In addition, when running two hiring boards, a peer or trainer board and a primary board, including the input from the peer board and having clear discussions over each applicant will motivate both boards with the feeling of involvement and appreciation. I have witnessed applicants hired when the oral board does not fully consider the peer board's decision and these trainees do not always do well.

The short answer on how to reduce expenses in this process is, there are very few ways you can cut corners in this process, and still have strong, viable candidates for hiring.

All Trainees Are Not Equal

Keep in mind that your trainees are not going to have the same education level, prior experience, or knowledge when they start. When hiring trainees with experience, you may realize additional savings. After receiving a positive report from their current agency, you may shorten the background, and agencies will skip a physiological exam when hiring a new employee in good standing with their current employer.

In Chapter 3, we discussed the mechanics of your training program in depth. Here I want to look at some individual traits and skills. Life experience is particularly important in the new hires' orientation. From all the investigations you have done to get the candidate to advance through the hiring process, they all have the same desire to work for you and successfully complete their training. Here are examples for your consideration:

> ➢ Anna had no public safety experience but a desire to be a 9-1-1 professional. She put herself through the local college program's 40-hour basic and 40-hour advanced telecommunicator school. The program also included EMD and some CAD exposure using the same programs we used in our PSAP. She was an extraordinary trainee and continues to be a fantastic dispatcher and trainer.

> ➢ Carla was a fire/EMS dispatcher for ten years with no police experience. After ten years, her familiarity with talk groups and mutual aid communications was strong in the region which helped strengthen our overall operation. She could teach our veterans about radios and the county/state protocols.

> ➢ Tim took early disability retirement as a police officer due to a motorcycle accident. He was young, in his forties, and still enjoyed helping people. Working as a part-time dispatcher was just what he was looking for, and we needed him. His training needs were just fire and EMS. He recently finally retired for good after a 20-year dispatching career.

> ➢ Judy's husband was a police officer and she worked as an administrative assistant for the police chief of one of our agencies we dispatched. She knew the local policies and

procedures for that community and was experienced dispatching police, fire, and EMS when it was just a single PSAP. Hiring her in the consolidated PSAP that had three additional communities was an easy transition to getting her fully on board.

➢ John graduated from a local high school and worked for two years in a metal shop. His desire and personal drive to perfection made him a great candidate. He was only 20 years old without much life or work experience, so he needed it all. The benefit of hiring him was his desire to do an excellent job for years to come. Sure, we had to get him extra classes outside of our CTOs and in-house training, but it had proven to be worth it. Great attitudes are contagious and that is what he brought to our agency.

So, with these examples, you see that your cost for training may not be equal as well. Applicants who have prior experience, knowledge and skills will cost less in terms of money to get on board. Others you may want to send to extra outside classes for more in depth training in particular areas such as customer service, police dispatching, fire dispatching and emergency medical dispatching, as examples.

Agencies across this country are facing staffing shortages. Organizations are using the same strategies expecting different results, which is insane. We all know that saying, "the definition of insanity is doing the same thing over and over expecting different results." Believe it! You need to reposition, rethink, restrategize and revisit what you think is etched in stone for hiring 9-1-1 dispatchers. The world has changed, and we need to do the same.

CHAPTER 6

Training Cycles and On-The-Job Burnout

We have touched on it and most have experienced it—the revolving door of the never-ending-training dilemma. For your entire staff, always in the mode of training new people is taxing and can lead to early burnout. This leaves leadership in a dilemma – if you don't hire to fill the spots, excessive overtime may cause burnout, constantly hiring and training, also leads to burnout. Lyra's 2022 workforce report revealed that 32% of those surveyed reported burnout in 2021, up from 29% in 2020. Burnout translates to resignations with a whopping 40% of respondents reporting they left their job because of burnout. The Mayo Clinic reports that job burnout is a "special type of work-related stress." The World Health Organization (Prior, 2019) has classified burnout as a legitimate medical diagnosis related to specific factors. Experts believe that it can be a root cause behind other conditions such as depression, substance abuse, heart disease, high blood pressure, even diabetes. While there are no clear directives to do this, regarding when to hire and when to pause, there are strategies that agencies can put in place to help current staff.

Choosing CTOs

One thing we have not touched on is how to choose a CTO. Consider this when opening the CTO selection process—while current staff members may be enthused about the opportunity of training, do they have the necessary experience and exposure to what occurs at a 9-1-1 center to provide the solid training your agency needs? Typical time on the job before being promoted to CTO status ranges from 18 months to three years, with an average of two years job experience.

The status as a CTO is a significant responsibility. Remember your CTOs are shaping the organization with how they train new hires. Good training equals solid dispatching skills. Consider the process for choosing CTOs to start with a letter of interest to be reviewed and interviewed by the leadership team. Help the CTOs to feel confident in what they are signing up for, what is expected, and what they expect will all be helpful aspects to the training program.

Things to consider is the performance of the CTO applicant. Has the person had any recent discipline? Is gossiping, rumor mongering, or poor behavior a concern? Remember if these are challenges for the applicant, the added responsibility of training is not a magic wand that changes it, chances are the stress of training (and it is stressful) will amplify those characteristics that are detrimental in the workplace.

After selecting the new CTO and before they are given their first trainee, make sure they have attended (and passed) a certified CTO course. Providing the new CTO with information on how the agency operates the CTO program and the expectation from the agency assists the new CTO to identify those topics during the certification class. Having knowledge of how the PSAPs training program operates eases their participation in the classroom discussions. Encourage them to take notes so they can remember any new processes that may prove beneficial to their team.

Remember, attendance and completion of a certified CTO class is important for your agency in terms of liability. Putting a new hire with someone who lacks training certification and has not received a thorough review of the PSAP training program will increase your liability exposure.

CTO Burnout

Your employees are your agency's primary asset. Preparing them for the job during their onboarding and training period is critical for your agency to ensure all involved can experience growth and success. A recent survey shows that 40% of employees leave organizations within the first year when they receive poor training (Periyasamy, 2022). While there is no specific data in a PSAP setting, if you couple the average statistic with the high stress and never-ending training loop, it can be even higher. Constant training is a strain on CTOs. Even those employees who enjoy training can begin to lose their luster after months of continuous training. With typical burnout symptoms of criticalness, cynicism, irritability, and difficulty concentrating, these are not traits you want to expose your current staff to and certainly not while they are training the newbie!

I have experienced constant training firsthand as a CTO and also watched my employees go through it as a director. Leaders must balance the push from current staff to get those seats filled with a strong awareness of CTO burnout. While the staff is tired of the overtime, tired of short-shifts, tired of training, communicating the education piece of why moving a little slower is crucial. In a perfect world, depending on your turnover rate you could hire, fill the empty seats, and give all involved a rest after a year (although technically speaking, in a perfect world turnover does not exist!). When I was a CTO, there was a time when my supervisor had me training two people at the exact same time. One was a little further in the process when I received the second. It was grueling and at the end of the day I was exhausted. The process went on for two months culminating in a full staff for another six months. The light at the end of the tunnel gave me the strength to continue, but what if there was no light? An on-going training cycle lasting months and years can deplete your CTO's ability to train or worse yet, to stay with your agency.

Number of Trainees

If you have three CTOs and two trainees, you can provide breaks within the training schedule. Consider that you are a smaller center and you have hired two new people. With three CTOs, it is challenging but embedding breaks provides down-time so that your CTOs are not training non-stop.

For example, using a simple Gantt chart or any other project management type tool, you can easily track the trainee's progress through phases as well as clearly see the assigned CTO, giving each (for this fictitious example) a six-week break. All the steps can be put in this tool, where the trainee will go in each step and with who, along with the projected time frame for each phase and task. If additional steps need to be added, it is as easy as an insert function on a spreadsheet, with the advantage of a tracking mechanism built in. Why a project management tool? Bringing on new employees and training them is a project, any leader and trainer will tell you that!

The number of trainees your agency brings on at one time is a leadership decision. Understanding the current staff's stress level is essential. Providing them with a four-week break between new hires will give the CTOs a much-needed rest. If you hear complaints from other staff who are qualified but refuse to train, you could always remind them how much faster filling the seats is if the agency had more trainers! Any volunteers?

CTO Recognition

How you recognize CTOs can help your qualified staff make the choice to go this route in their career.

Compensation for CTOs is difficult for agencies with budget shortfalls and leadership that may not understand the importance of this position. Compensation can include benefits such as increased pay during training, increased level of responsibility with a pay raise with or without a trainee, or a combination of these benefits. CTOs could also opt to receive compensation time if it is available for your agency. The drawback of comp time is that if your agency is already short-staffed, building up a comp bank will add to the shortages and compensatory time is a financial liability when working on budgetary plans so make it part of a full package planning. The critical issue here is appropriate compensation for your CTO staff. The job they do is vital to your agency and the service it provides for the public and first responders. Make sure they know how much you value their contribution.

As important as it is for CTOs to know how much leadership values their contributions, it is equally important that they have faith enough in leadership to accept a CTO position. This means your CTO program is designed to bring fully trained personnel into the PSAP. Ideally, the CTO program, in its development, included input and collaboration with the full CTO staff and consider including non-CTOs that are leaders in your organization. Significant time and effort have been put into every aspect of the program, from creating it, choosing the CTOs and mentors, and training everyone involved. There has also been significant use of the PSAPs resources and staff to bring out the best in the trainees. The CTOs want to know and have faith that leadership will support their decisions when a trainee is struggling. Ensure that the CTOs understand exactly what they need to do for documentation purposes - when goals are achieved and when they are not. Then when the CTO documents that a trainee is not thriving and reports to you that a performance improvement plan is needed or a significant incident and termination is recommended, work with the CTOs to help them document the situation and then follow through on their recommendations. Remind your CTOs what a vital role they fill in the organization and how much you count on their properly documented input. The program needs top leadership to support the vital CTO work. Without it the confidence in leadership will slip and with it, your program will falter.

Training Program

Leaders may make the mistake of believing they have *completed* the training program that they have just spent months creating. It's referred to as "this is my baby!" and any suggestions to correct or change are met with staunch opposition. What to do? First, pretend you have no toes, that way you will not feel anyone stepping on them. One of my favorite phrases that I use when someone wants to change something I have created is, "No worries, I don't have any toes, you can't step on them!" Then make sure the following actions and behaviors match the statement. When leaders are in creation mode, they can become so entrenched in the process that they lose sight of other things. Creativity is a gift, many in the PSAP career are gifted with creativity, surround yourself with them and allow for changes. Just like policies and procedures, the training program is a living, breathing document. The Wikipedia definition is one of my favorites, "A living document, also known as an evergreen document or dynamic document, is a **document that is continually edited and updated**." Your training program must continually update as technology advances. Processes change and you will discover the flow of information needs adjustment. So, edit it, revise it, and make it reflect the PSAP culture each member is striving for. One word of caution, once someone has been trained in any version of the program, make sure that version is retained. Follow your retention policy (and if you do not have one, make this your number 1 next step), retain it in digital or paper format, but keep these documents to protect your agency from future liability.

At this point, you may say, "future liability?" Why would not keeping a training document put liability on the agency? Think of this, you have a seven-year employee who makes a mistake, either blatantly or accidentally, and claims s/he learned to do "it" that way during training. Seven years ago, the training program was completely different, and the old program is long gone and although anyone can make a claim, without documentation stating otherwise, it does get messy trying to refute the claim. However, if the program that was used to train seven years ago was retained, showing that there are no directives to do "it" that way in the written document, will go a long way in reducing the mess.

Future CTO

With proper mentoring your agency can encourage internal growth in the organization at every level. Not to say that everyone is going to be happy about those who are promoted into positions of leadership but trying to operate with the end goal in mind is a great way to prepare your organization for leadership growth. Because of the many tasks involved in training, CTOs are considered, in some organizations, as a first line supervisor position. ONET online states that specific tasks for first-line supervisors in public safety are:

- Explain police operations to subordinates to assist them in performing their job duties.
- Train staff in proper work procedures
- Analyze information and evaluate results for the best solution (daily observation reports from a trainee fits here)
- Document/recording information
- Resolve (assist in) interpersonal conflicts

The task set fits the duties, but what of the skills? People First stated that a first line supervisor must have five essential skills (Calvert, 2018):

1. People skills
2. The ability to set and manage expectations
3. Communication
4. People development
5. Technical skills

Those lists sound just like the CTOs! Intentionally groom those dispatchers with the desired skill set already in place. Groom those dispatchers who may lack the essential skills but are teachable and can grow into the position. If you think of succession planning as putting people with the proper skills, education, and mind set to take your job, the first step is to identify the going-to-be-leaders in the organization and provide mentoring. Give them responsibilities such as mentoring. Mentoring is a critical piece for a successful organization and provides personnel with a pleasant environment to grow. (More on this in Chapter 7 under Mentoring and Succession Planning.)

Workplace Well-Being

There are shelves of books on workplace well-being. For the purposes of mentoring, hiring, and retaining, there are many things you can put in place in your PSAP, some may seem unrealistic, but proven to work in business settings.

In his book, *Life Force*, Tony Robbins (Robbins et al., 2022) provides a simple checklist to help longevity and health which I've paragraphed below. (See, *Life Force* for more details[28].)

- Hydrate – drink half your body weight in ounces of water each day.

- Eat foods close to their natural source – avoid processed carbs and meats.

- Decrease disease risk – consume one serving of broccoli and broccoli sprouts, cauliflower, brussels sprouts, or kale each day.

- Commit to a structured eating window – fast for 12-16 hours each day.

- Stay consistent with sleep.

- Get strong with 3 resistance training sessions per week.

- Strengthen your heart, lungs, and build endurance with 3 cardiovascular exercises per week, 20-30 minutes each.

- Use heat and cold as positive stressors to lower disease risks.

- Train your brain with breathwork and meditation for 5-20 minutes per day.

Environment

Plants

Plants are at the top of the list of things easily accomplished to establish a comfortable environment[27]. Since many PSAPs are without natural light, high quality silk plants may be best. The key to keeping them pleasant is to make sure they are dusted frequently. It will take less care to keep them clean than it would to keep them watered!

While it is true there are only so many things that can be done in a PSAP environment, it's the small things that can help with the atmosphere.

Lighting

Lighting in an area that is dependent on computer usage is critical. Lighting ergonomics for computer users is every bit as important as an adjustable desk and chair. Changing out the lighting can be an expensive task, especially if done correctly, but greatly reducing the eye strain helps the staff in the PSAP to avoid additional eye stress which can lead to vision impairment, as well as helping them to have less headaches, including migraines. Fluorescent lights are great for a cheap, energy saving solution, but very hard on the eyes. Exposure to fluorescent lighting (even the compact fluorescent lights - CFL) or bright overhead lights in a can cause eye strain and blurred vision, leading to the need for vision correction (glasses), headaches and migraines. Studies show that bad lighting—meaning the position/location, the quality, quantity, and color temperature can throw off an employee's mood, causing an off-the-chart mood swing for seemingly no reason after continuous exposure to improper lighting.

What can you do about this one? Reducing glare on the screen is an inexpensive and quick fix to start. Computer monitors should not be near the windows. Adjustable indirect light or light diffusers allow for the staff to adjust the lights to no brighter than necessary (keeping in mind that adjustable lights may also be a source of conflict between staff members). The indirect light reduces glare as well.

Blue light filters on the monitors will help your staff. Studies show that prolonged exposure to blue light is harmful and can cause permanent eye damage. Too dim or too bright of light will impact the body's natural circadian rhythms. While the soft yellow/white tones will not produce that bright white light associated with energy and productivity, it does provide an excellent option for completing tasks requiring mental stability as well as a relaxed atmosphere.

Last is the placement of the lights. Indirect lighting has greater flexibility within the room but making sure there are no lights placed where high screen glare occurs is imperative. Bringing in a lighting specialist to discuss each of these topics provides a great return on investment. A lighting specialist can provide your agency with an optimal solution, helping you to reduce the liability of poor lighting for the staff while increasing a welcoming and productive work environment.

Seating

The most essential functions in your center occur from a chair. Make sure your chairs are fully adjustable and long lasting. Seating companies will often bring demo chairs out and you can let your staff try them for a couple of weeks. Over the years I have visited many centers and talked to numerous PSAP directors/managers about chairs. Some centers have a chair room, where everybody has their own personal chair. Others have found a brand/style they like, and everyone gets the same chair, one chair per position. Still others have a variety of chairs for their staff to choose from. Unless your decision is to have one chair per person (very costly and you must have a lot of room) there will be some challenges with your chairs. Too big, too short, not comfortable, not breathable, and easiest to solve is the complaint that people do not want to sit on the chair after another has been sitting and has overheated. Personally, have you ever sat down on a seat after someone was sweating in it? Seriously, "yuck!" Easy solution, chair pads. Less expensive than one chair per person, and everyone who wants one is issued one. Thin and regular sized chair pads will eliminate the concern of sitting in a chair after a co-worker.

Nutrition

Working 8, 10, 12-hour shifts, throwing in overtime and you're up to a 16-hour shift, and snacks are inevitable. You cannot insist on healthy choices, but you can encourage it with a snack area offering healthy and nutritious options. Fruit, nuts, and other healthy snacks will encourage people to eat better. Also making sure the snack/kitchen area has a variety of ways to cook food such as an air fryer, microwave, stove/oven. This will allow people to bring their own food as opposed to ordering out. I have been known to stock a freezer with ice cream once a month during the summer. I included healthy options and those with sugar challenges always appreciated it.

Paid Time Off

It contributes to the administration's circling nightmare of trying to fill the seats, however, offering more benefit time than the standard bare minimum will provide your staff with time off to help ease the stress of the job.

Fitness

Standing desks, treadmills, and desk bicycles are becoming important commodities in PSAPs. Why, may you wonder? Employees may or may not get sufficient breaks while working their shift. The call volume may not allow anyone to get up and go for a walk or, if available, use a fitness center/onsite gym. Exercise does so much for mental health as well as physical health. Standing treadmill desks work by making a small treadmill platform that sits under the desk. Desk bicycles only work for adjustable desks, but employees can ride on the stationary bike while dispatching. In the high stress filled environment of a PSAP, offering programs to combat this while the staff is working will let them know that you value their health and contributions to the team. Fitness will also greatly improve productivity and output. Healthline.com states that research suggests endorphin release occurs after only 30 minutes of exercise. Exercise might include a walk, a bike ride, or more strenuous (not in the PSAP appropriate) exercise. For life in the PSAP, productivity and output mean less errors and less conflict and endorphins can help relieve pain, reduce stress, and cause a euphoric feeling. Studies show that you are likely to see more benefits from more exercise, and any amount is better than none.

Break Room

This is not a room to go to for eating per se. It is a room to go and relax, de-stress, and breathe deeply. In one PSAP I worked at, we called this room, "the cry room." Initially, it was nicknamed so because it was in an area that was behind what was a chapel where parents could take their children if they were crying. As time progressed, the PSAP employees stated that it was a cry room so they could go there and cry after a stressful situation. To outfit this room, management, staff, and union members worked together to create a warm and inviting room. A place to go if a mentoring session was needed, a peer-to-peer support chat was needed, or most frequently, a place to go and relax, close your eyes, listen to music, or even take a nap during your break. Certainly, a far *"cry"* from the break room I used in my early days of dispatching! "Back in the day" we had no break room, if anyone wanted to go and relax during a break, the best place was the locker room, and you could rest on the locker benches… something I did more times than I could count. The break rooms should have soft lighting, inviting wall decor, as well as comfortable furniture. Depending on the size of the room, consider including a bookshelf and TV. Many employees would love the opportunity to do some gaming on a break. While a gaming unit would be welcomed by many of the staff, the priority of a break room is to create a comfortable and quiet environment.

Do not expect any of these well-being suggestions to cure all of the challenges you may have with some of your PSAP staff. However, addressing workplace well-being from every angle within your organization has long stretching tentacles. Each of these listed items can enhance the employee's morale, which can help offset CTO burnout, and show all staff members from the newest to the most tenured, that they are valued and cared for.

CHAPTER 7

Continuous Review and Growth

"We never get any training." A statement you do not want your employees to feel, say, or experience. It is also a declaration you don't want to be stated in court during a civil suit against your agency. A statement you do not want employees to say during a disciplinary hearing. In fact, there is nothing good that will come out of that pronouncement, when stated due to an accurate reflection of the work environment. Continuous learning is the process of learning new skills and knowledge on an on-going basis. From formal training to in-house casual learning, the culture of your agency can be one that encourages employee involvement, self-initiative, and personnel taking on challenges for growth. Think of continuous training as exercise. The Mayo Clinic recommends 150 minutes of moderate aerobic activity or 75 minutes of vigorous aerobic activity each week—and here is the biggie—spread it out over the course of a week, not all in one day! If you want your staff to attend 16 to 24 hours of continuous education each year, consider spreading it out into 4- or 8-hour blocks (you can find some excellent educational classes that last one hour as well) over the year. Three 8-hour classes or two 8-hour classes and eight 1-hour sessions will provide your staff with continuous growth that they can put into practice throughout the year.

There is a difference between continuous learning and block learning. While both ways of learning offer updates and important information, block learning is closer to the concept of one-and-done learning. Meaning, employees are sent to classes once annually to receive all updates, new information, or refresher on current information. This training is better than nothing at all! Agencies have an easier time pulling people out of the schedule once per year, than offering training continuously. According to the Hewlett Packard studies, continuous learning is proven to make employees happy. Continuous growth opportunities show the employees that the organization cares about them. For individual employees, this type of learning process can help them find their passion in the career because it exposes them to different skills and development opportunities that they may not be aware of. My first 10 years in the field were full of on-the-job learning experiences, new friends, new concepts, no extra training. I didn't know about NENA, APCO, and the variety of other 9-1-1 related companies and topics until I accepted a job 70 miles away. I still remember the awe I felt the first time I went to a state APCO/NENA conference and when I went to a national conference, I was shocked at everything that was available. Throughout my tenure with the agency, I became more aware and involved of the training opportunities and I found that taking three to six classes per year felt more beneficial than three classes in a row or a one week-and-done training schedule.

Why is continuing education presented in a continuous manner more beneficial? Think of an athlete, amateur, semi-pro, or professional, no matter the level, athletes do not train once a month or even once before a game, they train continuously. The more training athletes do, the less chance they have of becoming tired during their game (or event). Training helps athletes mentally prepare for their games, if they do not prepare themselves physically before games, they may struggle with the needed mental preparation as well. Using the same comparisons in PSAP language—the more we attend training sessions as PSAP personnel, the better chances we have of processing calls for service with current information and knowledge. Training throughout the year helps emergency dispatchers be mentally prepared for their shifts, ready to answer any type of call for service that comes into the center. Repeated stress management classes, on a schedule to repeat every 2 to 4 years, as an example can help employees engrain those management techniques so that when (not if) they experience changes in their personal life, calls for service that go sideways, or a stress trigger call, they have the repeated training on techniques to handle the situation. Think of continuous training as a proactive approach to your leadership. As an example, classes addressing generational differences, morals and ethics, and customer service, as examples, are better for employees to attend *before* they have challenges in those areas. Sending an employee to a class focused on children and 9-1-1 before they take a call so that they have the knowledge and skills to manage a child caller, is better than sending them after they have made a mistake with a child caller.

I have heard, from other leaders, these top five popular myths when it comes to providing training for employees repeated as reasons not to train (Arun, 2021).

Myth One: Training is only for new hires and those with performance challenges.

Every employee will benefit from training and development for their personal growth and for the agency to reap the benefits of employee development. Specific training, as it pertains to the job, is needed to help them reach their potential level within the job specifics. But think of training as more than that, think of training as a way to increase job satisfaction by providing the employees with skills such as how to create a PowerPoint presentation, how to use spreadsheets. Skills that give them chances to use current technology, which will also further your succession planning plan!

Just make sure you are providing growth opportunities in areas where there is an interest or curiosity. Without that spark on the employee's part, it will be like forcing them to attend a social event, enforced fun, is never "fun"!

Myth Two: Collaboration and feedback are not necessary; employees can learn through lectures or presentations.

Children and adults alike want to be part of the learning process (although sometimes it sure doesn't feel like it when you hear...*silence*... after asking questions). By giving the group time to reach conclusions and work through peer-to-peer learning, the employees will retain more of what they are learning. A bonus to the instructor is that feedback provides information to tackle situations that may arise, which ultimately enhances the training program.

Myth Three: Training is only beneficial to the employees.

I call this, "stinkin thinkin!" Not only is a well-educated and trained staff beneficial to the employee, but regular documented training for all employees reduces liability for the organization. In addition, as earlier discussed, putting in place a training feedback system will give leadership and staff a method for learning what the employee learned and felt was important.

Myth Four: Online training programs are ineffective.

Prior to the 2020 pandemic, online training was underutilized. When the pandemic hit and shut down all non-essential functions where people gathered, training vendors developed online training programs to keep their doors open. The providers converted the previously established programs to online, to give employees the ability to continually receive training. Equature, for example, offers a variety of online training for employees at all levels. From one-hour webinars to multi-day classes, Equature has online training available. E-learning comes as part of the learning management that allows organizations to make resources available to employees, conduct assessments of the courses and provide certificates. Some online training is provided in "live" mode, meaning the student must be in front of their devices at a designated time. Other online training is pre-recorded and allows for the student to take the training at times best suited for them.

Myth five: Training is too costly to be continuous.

Think about this, organizing training programs once every three months can help employees hone their skills and improve consistency. How many zeros do you want to see your organization put on that check when the training program is proven to be ineffective in litigation? John Dewey said, "Education is not preparation for life; education is life itself." Life itself, for your employees, you, and your organization.

One last thing about education—Mirror Neurons. This concept is taking hold because it makes sense. Have you ever watched someone yawn, then find yourself yawning? I wonder who in reading this yawned just thinking about yawning? Mirror neurons are responsible for yawning when we see someone else yawn. They also act when we see someone sad, crying, smiling, and laughing. Mirror neurons allow us to learn through imitation. I have often heard the phrase, "Do what I say, not what I do." Sadly, that is not what really happens. When your employees see their leaders attending the same training they attend, making training a priority, the mirror neurons will kick in. Is leadership happy about the training or kicking and moaning? Leadership's approach to learning will be mirrored by the staff who are watching them. Mirror neurons will be an asset to your organization when you show happiness and optimism in your workplace. Throughout my tenure as a PSAP leader, I tried to be upbeat about whatever we were doing. Leadership can be hard at times, and I noticed (especially during my last days in the PSAP), that when I was sad, grouchy, annoyed, my staff's moods were reflected in how they treated each other, the customers, and the leaders. Mirror neurons will impact every part of the PSAP. As a leader, learning to control those emotional contagions (a process where a person (or group) can influence the emotions and behavior of another person or group) produced by mirror neurons will help you and your agency to be successful.

Mentoring and Succession Planning

Any time you can get outside, feel the sun, and enjoy the fresh air, is a good thing. One of the ways people enjoy being outside is in a garden. Flower garden or vegetable garden, it doesn't matter which one. You plant your seeds or seedlings, you water them, cultivate them, watch them grow. They need sunlight, they need to be weeded, they need special care from predators. If you do not weed them, the aggressive, unwanted plants (weeds) will overtake them. If you don't make sure they have proper amounts of water and light, they will shrivel up and die. If you don't protect them, the predators will destroy them. But when you provide the proper mixture of care, they will grow up strong.

From seedling to a strong plant, then what? You admire your work, even pat yourself on the back. You want to do more. Your plants are strong and healthy, perhaps you decide that the plant appears to have the potential to produce big crops, big flowers, or both. So, you add fertilizer to the mix. Some plants will explode with growth and become mature plants. Others will withdraw, cease to thrive and instead start wilting and begin to die, never to reach the potential you saw in them (at this point you regret patting yourself on the back). A few may just stay the same – steady growth (still good), but not the radical change you envisioned. Your survivors will go on to produce healthy crops, which will give you more seeds, and you can in turn sow those seeds during planting season, and the process continues.

Like gardening, succession planning, which includes mentoring, is a critical path within a leader's career. Growing leaders behind you ensures that your organization continues on the solid productive path your team has created after you've moved on. The newly appointed leaders will have more energy to expand and change because you have provided them with a strong base of fertile soil. You see, planting a garden is like mentoring others in that you are investing in the future and planning for the day when those mentored will explode with growth, becoming the next leaders in the organization.

To mentor means to be an advisor and coach, provide advice, guidance, and feedback. To be a mentee means one must have the desire and ability to be a follower. Until we learn to follow, it is difficult to be a good leader. Good leaders know that good followership means to be creative, outspoken, but not difficult and demanding (Slager, 2019). Good leadership is a basic requirement for cultivating good followership, and the best time to learn is when you're the subordinate. Good followership will get people noticed. Mentoring those with good followership abilities will provide your organization with people who have good instincts, good work ethic, and of utmost importance, good character.

To enhance the culture of your organization into one of mentoring and succession planning, the key is to follow the golden rule we all learned in kindergarten, do unto others as you would have done to you, or for this situation, do unto others what you want them to do unto others. You are a leader; eyes are watching you. When you fall, when you soar, the staff at your PSAP is watching how you meet conflict, change, mentoring, and promotions. You will fall, you will soar, no matter how much back patting occurs, these two things are going to happen. It is what you do with your failures and how you handle the successes that determine WHO you are. Your character, your ethics, and your "being." No matter what situation is facing you, be aware that sometimes one aspect of our being develops at the expense of others if we are not careful. This is not the culture you want to propagate when striving to hire and retain employees.

You hire a new employee and plant the seedling... oh, I mean, put the trainee into the work environment. You provide them with on-the-job training, you may appoint a mentor to help them maneuver through the trials of a new job. As trainees and probationary employees, you make sure they have the proper amounts of training, experience, and exposure to the others in the public safety profession so that they can develop strong. You try your hardest to protect them from predators, those who will steal their dreams and aspirations with the negative views of everything to do with the work environment. This can prove difficult because those negative forces who lurk behind the headsets in every PSAP can be deceptively convincing, especially to the newer employees.

Bottom-Up Approach

Your goal is to intentionally surround the trainees with positive influences. Upon successfully completing this goal, your released trainee is on their own and what do you know, this person has potential! Focused succession planning includes developing tools for staff's input to help improve their performance and work environment from every level. Identification of potential leaders from newest on up is what you want to strive for. Staff can provide insightful suggestions on how to improve the teamwork, professionalism, and general work environment simply by sharing ideas that would be fun to implement or items to purchase with a fresh perspective. This type of staff involvement can provide leadership with a vision of what the suggester could be like with a promotion. Are the ideas positive and insightful or do they lean toward negativity or pot stirring? As your leaders emerge at each level of your organization, mentoring may include clipping back your own wings and allowing the future leaders to grow. Just like a growing plant cannot reach its potential if it is smothered by the gardener, future leaders must have room to expand without others intervening so often that they lose the ability to become great. Look at this as an opportunity to allow them to soar with a safety net (that's you and your leadership team) to catch them when they falter (and they will).

As discouraging as it may be, you must continue the process of moving forward when the person who has so much potential leaves and goes to another agency. Be proud that your agency was able to groom and nurture a leader, even if they leave to lead. Not all people will bloom where they are planted. Some will bloom in another location. What a great moment! They are using the skills you taught them and going to make another agency better. Now your agency has a gap, and there is a feeling of loss. You lost a leader—someone you had invested in and worked with. What do you do? You talk about how great it is that someone who worked for you is working at an elevated level in another job, you congratulate them, you reflect on the positive attributes they brought to the agency before they left, and then you move on.

Not all the identified seedlings are going to make it. Some may lose their way, others may advance away, others will stay. The stronger your organization is with people within the succession planning process, the more seeds that can be planted, and the more people you will reach with positive growth. It is a true win-win scenario!

Encouraging Growth

Engagement and disengagement are two of the most crucial factors in an employee's success. Gallup research found that 83% of professionals would like to be involved in a mentoring program. But just 29% of workplaces offer mentoring programs. Mentoring programs are a simple way to help employees gain new skills and enhance their performance in the workplace. They provide support both on and off the job. As a manager, you can help employees by recognizing their strengths and providing them with guidance to help them grow. Providing opportunities for your employees' growth is another way you can increase engagement and reduce turnover. Here are tips on how to encourage employee growth and engagement.

Encourage Employee Growth and Development. Most managers know that employee retention is one of the top priorities for their department. But it can be difficult to create a workplace environment where employees feel valued and engaged. One of the best ways to build engagement and encourage growth is by encouraging professional development through mentorship. Studies show that mentoring has benefits for both mentors and mentees. And these benefits can spill over into the organization. Mentoring programs can help develop the leadership skills of both mentees and mentors, helping them to become better managers and better team members. Here is an incomplete list of the benefits that organizations can expect from implementing a mentoring program.

Develop Leadership Skills. One of the biggest benefits of the mentoring program is that it helps develop the skills of both mentors and mentees. Developing leadership skills is one of the most important things you can do for your employees and your business (Information Commissioner's Office, n.d.). A wonderful way to cultivate leadership abilities is through mentorship. Studies have shown that mentees are better prepared to take on leadership roles when they complete a formal mentoring program. Mentor your mentees with the end goal focused—the potential you see in them and their aspirations.

Develop Business Knowledge. Another great benefit of mentoring programs is that they help develop knowledge about the 9-1-1/PSAP as a career among participants. A recent study showed that businesses that use a mentoring program experienced a 75% decrease in staff turnover and a 70% reduction in training costs. Even though these statistics were gained from the private business industry, they show that investing in your people has a huge payoff in business. Business knowledge through formal training can be a turning point for mentees who are training to be a CTO, supervisor, or director. These formal classes are available in venues using face-to-face.

Strengthen Work Relationships. One of the most rewarding things about mentoring is that it strengthens work relationships across the organization. The more your team members feel like they are part of a team, the more likely they are to stay engaged and motivated. Mentoring is an important means to build camaraderie across teams, other shifts, and an enhanced environment.

Promote Career Development. Research shows that people who participate in formal mentoring programs are more satisfied with their jobs. The mentors and mentees in these programs feel more energized, motivated, and productive at work. They are less likely to leave the company and pursue other opportunities. It is a fact that successful people in the corporate world started out as mentees. If you want to be successful in your career, mentoring is a fantastic way for you to gain the experience you need to advance your career.

Reduce Employee Turnover. Another big benefit of mentoring programs is that they help reduce employee turnover. People who participate in mentoring programs are usually more satisfied in their jobs and therefore less likely to look for a new job or leave the company to pursue other opportunities. In addition, employees who are engaged in a mentoring program are more productive and more engaged than employees who are not involved. This improves the quality of their work and increases the overall productivity of your PSAP.

Taking a closer look at these benefits, a formal mentoring program can make key differences within your PSAP or public safety organization. Here are key benefits of using this type of program:

Team building. One of the primary things a mentor can do is to build rapport and trust with their mentees. This helps strengthen the relationships between the teams in the organization and encourages open communication and collaboration.

Retention. Research shows a link between mentorship and retention. Employees who are mentored are more likely to stay with the organization for a longer period than those who are not involved in any mentoring programs.

Teamwork. A formal mentoring program gives your employees an opportunity to interact with other members of your organization who share similar goals or interests. It helps team members develop a deeper connection with one another and promotes teamwork and collaboration across the organization.

Knowledge sharing. By giving your employees the chance to learn from others with experience or knowledge in different areas of the business, you can help them gain valuable knowledge and develop the skills they need to advance their careers and make a positive contribution to the company.

Improved morale. Research shows that employees who participate in a mentoring program are more satisfied with their jobs than those who don't participate. This can lead to increased loyalty and motivation within the team, which helps boost productivity and improve the overall business climate.

Recruitment. Successful mentoring programs can help organizations attract new team members who are attracted to positive workplace environments and high-functioning teams. When people see that your organization has a mentoring system in place, it will give them a better sense of what it is like to work at the PSAP and better prepare them for what is to come on their first day of work.

Improved communication. The mentor-mentee relationship can go a long way toward improving communication between teams and employees in an organization. Sharing experiences with their mentors can help employees better communicate with one another and build stronger relationships within their respective teams. Mentoring programs can boost morale in the workplace by giving employees the opportunity to interact with and learn from people who have experience in different roles within the organization. Employees also can form closer bonds with each other and develop a sense of belonging to their team and their workplace. A study published in the Harvard Business Review found that employees who participated in a mentoring program were significantly more likely to stay at the company for three years or longer. The same study found that participation in a mentoring program was linked to an 18% increase in engagement. In a public safety environment, increased engagement equates to a better ability to cope with the job stress and take advantage of healthy outlets. By enabling employees to connect with more experienced colleagues and build relationships outside of the PSAP, mentoring programs can increase overall job satisfaction and encourage a greater sense of belonging to the company.

Learning and development. People look to mentorship to advance their careers and learn new skills. In fact, more than 70% of people surveyed by Forbes said they wanted access to a mentor to help them with their career plans. Mentors can serve as invaluable sources of information and learning for employees, helping them to identify opportunities at their company and advance in their careers. Many organizations encourage mentees to use the knowledge they have gained through their mentoring relationships to apply for promotions and leadership positions within the company.

Better decision-making. Mentorship is an excellent way for employees to improve their decision-making skills. When employees have the chance to learn from people with more experience, they get the chance to gain insights and ideas that can help them make better decisions about their work. This can have a positive impact on their performance and the quality of their work. Keep in mind that mentoring is different from training. Employees can be involved in a mentoring program while they are still in training and the mentoring continues after training ends. For example, a mentor can help her mentee identify valuable skills or strengths that he may not have previously considered and help him capitalize on those assets to make himself a more effective employee.

Higher performance. By providing employees with an opportunity to learn from an experienced colleague, a mentoring program can also help them improve their performance at work. When employees can build relationships with more experienced colleagues and receive advice on how they can do their work more effectively, they can become more motivated to perform at their best. This can lead to greater job satisfaction and increased employee productivity in the workplace.

Agency-wide improvements. Another benefit of a mentoring program is that it can help improve communication within an organization. Employees who participate in a mentoring program have the opportunity to gain experience both from their mentors and their mentees. They can learn effective communication techniques from their mentors and see how to apply these techniques to their own work situations. In addition, the mentoring relationship allows them to share their ideas and insights with their mentees and learn from each other.

Higher job satisfaction. Another potential benefit of mentorship is that it can increase job satisfaction among employees. Mentors provide guidance and support to their employees, which can help them feel more fulfilled and engaged at work. The relationship can also provide them with a sense of purpose and help them develop skills useful throughout their careers.

Employee retention. Companies that invest in their workforce by providing opportunities for growth and development often see positive results in terms of employee retention. Studies have shown that encouraged and supported employees who grow throughout their careers are more likely to stay with the organization long-term and develop loyalty for their employer.

Nurturing a culture of learning. Mentorship programs can also be beneficial to organizations by helping to establish a culture of learning within the organization. For new employees, this can help them adjust to their new role more quickly and effectively. For more experienced employees, it can provide an opportunity to reflect on their strengths and weaknesses and help them identify areas for growth and improvement.

Future leaders. Finally, mentorship can also benefit organizations by preparing future leaders within the organization. By giving newer employees the opportunity to interact with and learn from more experienced employees, companies can encourage the development of valuable leadership skills within their organization.

Stay Interviews

A stay interview, what is that you may ask? Is it an interview you have once someone has notified you that they are leaving as in, please stay? Not even remotely correct. Before you begin conducting stay interviews, be prepared to listen and take notes. Notes that will capture key points, important quotes, and emotional words (Finnegan, 2018). In the PSAP profession, we are taught that active listening is a key skill, and we must learn it early in our career or we will not be successful. For stay interviews, active listening is no less important, you need to listen without being

107

distracted and thinking of the next question you want to ask, just focus on the words and the meaning of what is being said. This type of interview focuses on what can be done to help retain the employees before they tell you they are leaving. The interview can be scheduled when there are indications that a good employee is considering leaving. You want to determine the why behind their thoughts and during this process. It allows you to address issues upfront in an open discussion, with the employer being consistent and transparent. Forbes recommends focusing on making the interview personal, learning about who the employee is, what inspires them and what they want outside of work. This, when used appropriately, will help the organization support the employee as a whole person. Questions that focus on the employee, what they've learned, and what they want to learn in a work environment will help you understand if they are ambitious to advance, learn more, or work and go home. Find out what they look forward to each day during their commute to work and why they have stayed there up to this point. This question may surprise employees because they are prepared for "Why do you want to leave." Asking them the opposite is a good way to look at the positive side of the work environment. You may have to help them along by asking some probing questions such as:

- Is that the only reason you stay or are there others?
- Which other jobs here are of interest to you?
- What skills or training do you think you need for those jobs?

This should not be a marathon interview. Your goal is to probe into the employee and find out what keeps them engaged, what are their career desires and ambitions. Keep it to five primary questions, although you most likely will have follow up questions to those five. Close the interview by asking the key question similar to:

What can I do to make the job better for you?

This question is not meant to be a verbal contract between the two of you. It's meant to be a starting point—a place where you and your good employee can work toward a goal together. The answers to this question may bring in a plethora of answers along with some not so constructive feedback directed at the organization or leadership. Ultimately as the interviewer you must avoid becoming defensive. If you defend yourself or the agency, word will spread that you are unable to take feedback and your venture to keep a good employee will be the last attempt made. The stay interview process will be a retain tool you will be able to keep in your tool kit. Keep it positive, accept the feedback in whatever form it is presented and find elements within that can be improved, then move forward. Your staff is watching and will appreciate your efforts.

Continuous Learning

Continuous learning is the ongoing expansion of knowledge and skill sets. In addition to PSAP specific educational classes, other types of learning are beneficial for an agency. An avid believer in education, I earned a bachelor's and master's degree while working full-time in the PSAP and raising my children. Not an easy task but in striving for my goals, I knew the positions I wanted often required a degree. The degrees were instrumental in promotions, leadership/management positions, and opening up the doors that led me all over the United States. When I started writing this section my purpose was to provide encouragement for advanced educational degrees. However, after researching this a bit, I am adjusting that advice. The U.S. Bureau of Labor Statistics predicts the number of jobs requiring a bachelor's degree will increase by almost 10% between 2016 and 2026. In a report by the Harvard Business Review (HBR), 26 million job postings were analyzed and they discord that 6.2 million middle-skill jobs are at risk of what is termed degree inflation. A Forbes report shows that over the past few years, companies like Google and IBM, have decided to remove degree requirements from roles where a degree was not essential (Siler, 2022). Hiring a workforce with educational diversity has reaped benefits for companies across the country.

Continuous learning can occur through methods other than college. Trade schools may offer programs for a human resource specialist or a project manager, both examples can be beneficial for PSAP leadership. Special skills (such as spreadsheets, presentations) are essential for leadership at any organization. Encouraging growth in these areas can be a great benefit to your agency at all levels.

Liability

Liability is a factor of public safety that most leaders and organizations are familiar with. Many years ago, I saw a pictorial demonstration of how to reduce liability. It was a simple picture with a person under an umbrella, safe from the rain. On the umbrella was listed all the authority that you are under—policies, procedures, protocols, chief, city council, board of commissioners, state law, federal law, etc. The point was if you stay under the authority of those in authority over you, your liability risk is always diminished. I have held on to that idea for years. Liability concerns face each individual and organization when the policies, procedures, and protocols are not followed. Sometimes agencies get into a trick bag of not training due to personnel and/or budgetary shortages. The best quote I ever heard on holding back spending was from the City of Port Huron Police Department's Chief William (Bill) Corbett. He used to say frequently, "Well, we need funding for [fill in the blank]. They can either pay now and make the purchase or pay later in the lawsuit, but eventually they'll pay." Chief Corbett's statement was made to highlight the point of what happens when agencies don't provide the proper tools for public safety to do their jobs. Pay now—make the purchase and train the staff. Pay later—you'll pay more in a lawsuit, lose public trust, and you'll still need to make the purchase and train the staff. Over the years that I knew him, before his retirement and passing, he pointed out many situations where this mindset was accurate. Liability cannot be avoided, but it can be minimized. Once public trust is lost, the recovery for trust is long and painful. More complaints will be made. Under increased scrutiny, staff experience higher stress levels and tend to make more mistakes than before. As the cycle continues, it is difficult to stop it (Craig, 2016).

Training Program

The training program is the foundation of your organization. The misconception about training programs is that the training is complete when releasing the new trainee from the program and on his/her own. This thinking puts the agency at risk. Similar to how your initial training program is well structured and documented, ongoing training through a quality improvement program must also be structured and documented. Regular training and review of each policy and any revisions is imperative. If it is not written, it didn't happen. You may know beyond any doubt that employees have been trained and reviewed the policies regularly, but if you don't have documentation with their initials/signatures/dates, then you have no proof.

Planning out annual training for your staff will fit in nicely with your annual budget preparations. Using a quality assurance (QA) program, you can identify areas where the staff needs additional training each month or quarter. The specifics of what will be trained, as a result of the QA program, do not have to be identified in this initial training phase as much as a space reserved throughout the year for the training. For example, through case review, listening to recordings of phone and radio, you determine that your staff are missing address verification. These quality improvement (QI) sessions can be short, 15 minutes of information, and delivered in a variety of formats, followed by a brief two to five question quiz to verify understanding of the material.

- In person training is just that—going over the material face-to-face with the teams. The goal is to have all teams trained within one week of each other.

- A written document with a mini quiz distributed through email or supervisors. Give the employees a due date to read and return the quiz.

- A self-recorded video with a PowerPoint type presentation that employees can view at any time within the timeline provided.

Other training can be better defined in the pre-planning phase. Are there any certifications required for the upcoming year? If so, put it on the schedule. Are there any areas where certain staff members could use additional training such as stress management or managing specific call types, put it on the schedule. Lastly, ask the staff what kind of training they would like to attend, making sure they understand that they may not get to attend that specific training (due to availability, location, etc.).

Document your on-going training program process, just as you would your training program for new hires. This will not only ensure you have a sufficient budget for the training, but it will also keep you focused with a clear path of your progress.

You may wonder what this has to do with liability, hiring and retaining employees. Specific documented work-related training as well as personal care training (wellness, stress management type training) protect the agency from lack of training claims while empowering and engaging current staff. This provides a culture of growth and higher job satisfaction. When people experience a positive culture and high job satisfaction turnover is reduced. Everyone wins with well-defined and engaging training.

And remember when preparing for the upcoming year, the leadership team from top to bottom will benefit from regular training as well!

When They Leave

When I left all four of the PSAPs I worked for, I never had an exit interview (EI), yet there were many topics I thought would have been interesting to cover if there had been an opportunity for those discussions. Even when we know why an employee is leaving, there may be information that can be gleaned in an EI that would otherwise be missed. The EI should be the cumulation of regular conversations on how to improve and changes that can or must be made. The Harvard Business Review states that the practice of conducting an exit interview can be a powerful tool to use in retention (Spain & Groysberg, 2016). Asking how the employee was helped to be effective in the job, in building a successful career, in achieving a fulfilling life, are questions we may not have answers to from other conversations. There are differing views on who should receive an EI, but in a tight job market the safest and most effective method is to have a mandatory EI for all exiting employees. In some cases, the departing employee is leaving because he/she was not successful in the training program. For these employees, finding out about the experiences can help refine your processes. During the interview, you can determine what the employee's perceptions were about the work itself, what they felt about the training program, the trainer's and leadership team's effectiveness, and any issues relating to human resources (HR). These topics can help you refine your hiring and onboarding processes for future hires if there are any gaps.

For non-probationary employees, the goal of an EI is still to determine if there are any issues relating to HR, leadership's effectiveness, and the perceptions about the work itself. This is also a time to solicit feedback for the employee's ideas for improvement in the areas he/she feels there are deficiencies.

The goal of the EI is to use the information once it's gathered. An effective EI program can be measured by the positive changes it generates. When Harvard Business conducted a survey on the changes brought about by the EI process, fewer than one third of businesses could cite an example of any changes. Perhaps the data is not quality data. One suggestion to support this is based on who is doing the interview. If the boss is doing the interview and the employee feels the boss is the problem, are they really going to state that as the reason for their departure? Most likely they will not because they want a positive reference. An effective interviewer is an outside agency or third party. Most employees feel comfortable talking openly about their experiences in this situation without fear of retaliation.

The last item in an effective EI is the timing. Experts argue that the perfect timing is before the last week when the employee has mentally checked out, which would leave it during the first week of a two-week notice. Other experts argue that the first week is too emotional and the best time for an exit interview is two to three weeks post-employment. When emotions have calmed down and the employee is away from the environment. These interviews can be conducted by phone, in person, or in a virtual environment. Some organizations will also conduct a second post-employment EI one or two months following the last day with a mailed questionnaire, either electronically delivered or post-paid return envelope. They have found that these second EI's revealed information that the first one had shown no indication of.

Conducting an EI will help you improve your organization. They are not always comfortable when receiving feedback, but when sifting through the emotion, there are frequently nuggets of truth where improvements can be made. An article in Forbes even coaches people to "zip the lip" ... because HR doesn't *really* want to hear anything (Hannon, 2015). Your job, when you hear *anything, is to* view it constructively and not retaliate. One form of retaliation is when future employers do a background check, the EI should not come up as a negative toward the former employee – sometimes this is referred to as a form of blackballing. If there are any areas where the organization can improve, use them; if not, move on. Continual improvement will assist your agency in creating a culture of retention, helping you to shatter the turnover ratio that threatens to destroy organizations. An exit interview, used as a standard tool, can strengthen the bond between employees and the organization because the employees believe that the company demonstrates authentic concern for their professional well-being.

CHAPTER 8

Accreditation

Let me start by dedicating this chapter to Justin Hoslet. Without his help, his drive, and our shared vision and goal of achieving Accreditation (and then re-Accreditation), our PSAP would not have been able to reach the achievement. He excelled with energy and took hold of my dream, made it his, and worked by my side to make it a reality. Becoming an Accredited Center of Excellence was one of the pinnacles in my career and I will always be grateful to him for his dedication to excellence and the goals we laid out.

From the moment when I first heard about having the PSAP accredited, I was hooked on achieving the goal, however it still took three different agencies, an outstanding dispatch staff, close to 24 years and a very dedicated employee to come alongside me and help achieve that goal. Accreditation can seem like a waste of time and money if you focus on time and money. Achieving accreditation from any of the accrediting entities is not easy. It takes a lot of documentation, excellent quality assurance and improvement processes, strong policies, procedures, and protocols, backing of the governing body and most importantly, an excellent staff. All three of the places I worked where accreditation was a goal, the staff was hard working and dedicated, and I wanted to showcase them to the community. Accreditation takes a lot of focused attention and until I was with an agency where we had the available staffing to assist with that focus, accreditation remained a vision for the organization, a goal. When you achieve accreditation, it means you have staff that excel in their performance, month after month. The agency I worked for when we achieved the goal had all those factors in place. From the time I achieved my first leadership position, I always said the leaders of the organization can be whoever they are, but it's only when the line-level staff shine that a leader can shine as well.

Why would you want your agency to become accredited? What's the value for your organization, the agencies you serve, and the public? Some of the values are not quantifiable. It's the feeling of pride and accomplishment that the employees experience. While it certainly looks good for the agency, it's more about the outstanding performance of the telecommunicators. It's the pride the agencies you serve will have because they understand the work and adherence to the 3 P's (Policy, Procedures and Protocols) that was required by the employees to get there. The agencies that achieve accreditation are showing the citizens that their agency will provide the highest level of care and professionalism. The International Academy of Emergency Dispatch (IAED, 2022) states that there are a broad range of benefits that include (but are not limited to), increased visibility and recognition for your agency's role in community service as well as assistance with litigation and liability management. The IAED also reports that for some agencies with accreditation status, recruitment and retention rates are higher because the agency is showing that their work truly matters. The Commission on Accreditation for Law Enforcement Agencies (CALEA, 2022) states that the accreditation process helps to improve the delivery of public safety services by maintaining and providing proof of adherence and maintenance to the professional standards. The accreditation process ensures that the agency has current equipment and training for personnel, and it fosters community awareness with transparency and open dialogues.

When agencies hire new employees, they will go through the four stages of learning, that is unconsciously incompetent, meaning they don't know what they don't know. Training at this stage is tough because the CTO asks, do you have any questions? The trainee doesn't have a clue what they don't know so they say no. Then the trainee progresses and just bombs new skills. This phase is referred to as the consciously incompetent. The trainee knows that they do not know. Questions are more frequent at this stage and those eager to learn will want to know how to become competent. Competency is achieved in the third phase. Consciously competent employees know that they know, but they may need to double check it. This stage for the employee's knowledge and skill growth is when the person is actively learning and growing, and you can see it in the performance. Confidence levels are rising, and the employee is becoming comfortable with the skills and tasks. Unconsciously competent is the goal! The employees know that they know, and they don't need to verify for basic and advanced level tasks. They are good at doing what is right when procedures are resting in a gray area, they function in the mastery range of their career. While it is possible to slip in and out of the unconsciously competent phase, for those who have a passion for growing and learning, it rarely occurs. As a leader, working hard to provide the best for the agency, being aware of the consciously incompetent *who are aware and don't strive to learn* can help you catch problems early. This close attention to detail will encourage those unconsciously competent and consciously competent employees that the agency cares about them, their performance, and their success. Knowing these steps is a must for leadership, from the CTO leaders to the highest-level leader.

Agencies achieving accreditation have employees primarily working in this fourth learning phase. They also have employees who meet the rarely discussed fifth phase, described by Examine Existence (EE Editors, 2019) as the consciously competent of the unconsciously competent. This high functioning skill set is held by those who use their mastery of dispatching and public safety knowledge to help others achieve the same, these employees are your CTOs.

Accreditation Choices and Processes

There are choices when accreditation is your goal. The following choices should not be considered a comprehensive list, however it is provided to give you an idea of what is available. For agencies using the protocol system through the IAED, you can become accredited in one or all three of the disciplines, EMS, Fire, and Law. There is also CALEA, initially a law enforcement accrediting agency, CALEA incorporated the 9-1-1 center into the law accreditation process and then created a separate PSAP specific accreditation process. Accreditation processes vary from state to state, as well. States such as Virginia and Kentucky developed through processes for checks and balances for 9-1-1 centers. Check with your state and see if there are any statewide programs available for accreditation of your PSAP. In addition to a full PSAP accreditation, APCO has an accreditation process specifically for PSAP training programs and the Federal Law Enforcement Training Accreditation (FLETA) has a law enforcement training program.

The processes used during the accreditation review will vary depending on the agency used to achieve accreditation. The accrediting agency will review all written documents and require proof of compliance, may listen to recordings, visit the PSAP to verify compliance with safety standards and chat with staff, and provide feedback before, during, and after the review. The accrediting body will have the knowledge of state and national best practices, local policies, procedures, and protocol and they will verify how they are incorporated into the agency's daily actions.

Some of the best practice standards are available to help agencies meet the Accredited Standards Developer (ANSI) standard. One document outlining minimum training guidelines for telecommunicators can be found on the National Emergency Number Association website at: www.nena.org/page/Standards (NENA, 2014). This project was finalized in 2014 with input from 18 organizations across the United States.

Other specific example of these areas, not in any order, will include (but may not be limited to) these areas:

- Policies, Procedures and Protocols

  Staffing

  Answering process

  Phone call statistics

  Radio usage process

  Call for service statistics

  Security review - includes physical and digital

  - ★ NENA Standard 54-001 / Communications Center / PSAP Daily Personnel Operations Model Recommendation addresses basic rules of conduct and behavior.

  - ★ NENA Standard STA-021.1-2020 addresses the Model Recommendations for Call Answering Processes.

  - ★ NENA-STA-020.1-2020 - 9-1-1 Call Processing Standards

- Training Program

  Review of annual training plan, individual employee's received training. There are specific training standards available for references. Missing and Exploited Children, TDD/TTY, TCPR, PSAP & Railroad Interactions Standard, and Human Trafficking, as examples. Some specifics to help when establishing or refreshing current procedures can be found here:

★ NENA-STA 011/1-2021 is an ANSI Accredited NENA Standard for 9-1-1 Professional Education Recommendations.

★ NENA also supplies a Recommendation Plan for NG9-1-1 for Elected Officials and Decision Makers

- Quality Assurance (QA) and Quality Improvement (QI) program

  Includes reviewing copies of cases previously reviewed for QA

  QI training

  Consistency in program

  ★ APCO/NENA ANS 1.107.1-2015 Establishes recommended standards for QA/QI Programs in the PSAP.

- Technology and Security

  Making sure the PSAP is equipped with the proper technology and that it is up to date will be reviewed during an accreditation process. The security of the organization is also a factor. Security reviews will be conducted to ensure that all aspects of security, both physical and digital, are in compliance.

Understanding the reasons to become accredited is helpful to keep working toward the goal. Although the Better Business Bureau (BBB) (Kraus, 2022) accredited private businesses only, they incorporate eight areas to evaluate a company's rating. Most of these areas, although they have a different description from the public safety standards, mirror the goal of any accreditation process. The BBB goals with PSAP descriptors are:

- Building trust with your customers. In public safety, customers include everyone who has contact with the PSAP at any level.

- Truthfulness/Honesty. Whatever you say you do, follow through with. A high-quality characteristic and one that should be the foundation of the PSAP.

- Transparency - While there are confidential documents and processes within a PSAP and public safety, operating with open communication to the public, employees, and those served by the PSAP will reduce criticism and suspicion.

- Honoring promises - Answering the phone with compassion, dispatching with professionalism are duties that must be performed each day. Honoring the duty with the highest quality of service meets this standard.

- Being responsive - Answering the radio, responding to inquiries.

- Safeguarding privacy - What is the security like in your PSAP? Are the employees safe and the data safeguarded with security measures in place to ensure information is protected? Do you have a storm plan in place?

- Doing business with integrity - Approach all interactions with integrity and good faith, avoiding actions that reflect unfavorably on the PSAP and 9-1-1- profession.

Accreditation may not be for everyone because of a variety of circumstances, however if it is of interest to you or your agency, set your goal to achieve it. As you go through the process you are helping your PSAP at every level by showing how professional the PSAP staff really is. It may take you longer than you ever thought it would, be harder than you thought it could, and provide more worth than you imagined.

CONCLUSION

Ready to Respond and Retain

Begin With the End in Mind

From the Great Resignation to successful hiring practices, the process may seem simple from an outside perspective, but anyone in public safety knows these processes can be challenging. These suggestions may represent significant change for the agency. The popular idiom states that you should cross that bridge when you get to it. Meaning when you come to a problem, solve it (on a side note, the idiom's origins are not entirely clear. It's thought to have originated in a book by Henry Wadsworth Longfellow, *The Golden Legend*, in 1851). Given this, you may be thinking you will address the procedures you have in place regarding hiring practices to first, first responder ready when you need to. The challenge with that is, if you want to cross the bridge and have it not fall over, you have to understand the "why" behind the "what" and "how."

There are very few, if any, with perfect protocols, procedure, and policies solidly in place. That doesn't mean we can't strive to achieve that goal. Shifting the recruiting efforts and hiring techniques can incentivize people to apply to your agency. Training, review, and growth shifts will make the agency appealing to those looking in, and those already in place. Always striving to raise the standards of quality may make the task a little more difficult, but the product of that increased standard and practice will show itself in your staff, from the hiring process to the floor. Changes you make today can begin to show in as little as one year, when you give it a full twenty-four months you can change the entire culture of your organization.

APPENDIX

Daily Observation Report Examples

Performance Improvement Plan

<AGENCY> Performance Improvement Plan (PIP)	
Employee Name:	
CTO Name:	
Plan Start Date:	
Plan End Date:	
Description of the underperformance:	
Purpose/aim of the PIP:	

Improvement Objectives: What specifically must the individual do to improve their performance to meet expected standars?	Success Criteria: What are the expected standards of the performances? What actions must be completed to know if the standards are met?	Additional Details: Is there additional development or support required for the individual to achieve the expected standards?	Review Schedule - Dates of progress improvement objectives to be reviewed.	Objective Outcome - When will the final review of the plan be undertaken. What is the final outcome? What actions will be taken if expected outcome is not met?
[Enter improvement objective 1]	Detail success criteria for improvement objective 1	Additional support and details required to succed in achieving improvement objective 1	Detail dates when progress will be reviewed and by whom.	Detail the specific outcome. Detail the specific consequences if the invidual does not achieve improvement
Enter improvement objective 2	Detail success criteria for improvement objective 2	Additional support and details required to succed in achieving improvement objective 2	Detail dates when progress will be reviewed and by whom.	Detail the specific outcome. Detail the specific consequences if the invidual does not achieve improvement
<...>	<...>	<...>	<...>	<...>

Overall outcome when plan objectives are achieved/ not achieved: [Enter overall outcome / consequences at end of Performace Improvemet Plan when plan is / is not completed satisfactorily by the plan end date]

Supervisor: _____ Date: _____

Dispatcher Daily Observation Report

ᔕ Equature

Dispatcher Daily Observation Report   Day: _____

CTO Name	Emp #	Trainee Name	Emp #

Rating Instructions: Rate observed behavior using the scale below. Comment on the most and least satisfactory performance of the day. Comment on any behavior you wish, but a specific comment is required for ratings of "1" or "7". Check "N.O." box if behavior is not observed. If trainee fails to respond to training, check "N.R.T." box and comment.

Assignment or Reason for No Evaluation

RATING SCALE

Not
Acceptable   Acceptable   Superior

CATEGORIES

							NO	NRT	RT	CATEGORIES
1	2	3	4	5	6	7				**APPEARANCE**
1	2	3	4	5	6	7				1. General Appearance
										ATTITUDE
1	2	3	4	5	6	7				2. Acceptance of Feedback
1	2	3	4	5	6	7				3. Attitude Towards Job
1	2	3	4	5	6	7				4. Assumes Responsibilities
										KNOWLEDGE
1	2	3	4	5	6	7				5. Knowledge: Department & Section Manuals
1	2	3	4	5	6	7				6. Knowledge: Emergency Resources & References
1	2	3	4	5	6	7				7. Knowledge: Codes
1	2	3	4	5	6	7				8. Knowledge: Military Time & Phonic Codes
1	2	3	4	5	6	7				9. Knowledge: Maps, City Geography, Boundries
1	2	3	4	5	6	7				10. Knowledge: Districts, Areas & Neighborhoods
1	2	3	4	5	6	7				11. Knowledge: Criminal & Civil Law
1	2	3	4	5	6	7				12. Knowledge: CCIC & NCIC
1	2	3	4	5	6	7				13. Knowledge: CAD
1	2	3	4	5	6	7				14. Knowledge: Retention
										PERFORMANCE
1	2	3	4	5	6	7				15. Proper Use & Operation of Equipment
1	2	3	4	5	6	7				16. Telephones: Listens & Comprehends
1	2	3	4	5	6	7				17. Telephones: Control of Situation/Voice Control
1	2	3	4	5	6	7				18. Telephones: Collection of Information
1	2	3	4	5	6	7				19. Telephones: Organization/Computer Input
1	2	3	4	5	6	7				20. Telephones: Problem Solving & Decision Making
1	2	3	4	5	6	7				21. Telephones: Calls for Servic/Non-Stress Conditions
1	2	3	4	5	6	7				22. Telephones: Calls for Service/Stress Conditions
1	2	3	4	5	6	7				23. Telephones: Mechanics
1	2	3	4	5	6	7				24. Radio: Listens & Comprehends Radio Traffic
1	2	3	4	5	6	7				25. Radio: Copies & Returns Requests on Data
1	2	3	4	5	6	7				26. Radio: Articulation of Transmissions
1	2	3	4	5	6	7				27. Radio: Problem Solving & Decision Making
1	2	3	4	5	6	7				28. Radio: Allocation of Manpower
1	2	3	4	5	6	7				29. Radio: Prioritization of Traffic
1	2	3	4	5	6	7				30. Radio: Non-Emergency Traffic
1	2	3	4	5	6	7				31. Radio: Emergency Traffic
1	2	3	4	5	6	7				32. Radio: Prioritizing Calls for Service
1	2	3	4	5	6	7				33. Radio: Attention to Officer Safety
1	2	3	4	5	6	7				34. Radio: Appropriate Use of Codes/Procedures
1	2	3	4	5	6	7				35. Radio: Backup Systems/Manual Cards
										RELATIONSHIPS
1	2	3	4	5	6	7				36. Relationship with Citizens
1	2	3	4	5	6	7				37. Relationship with Department Members

TOTAL R.T.: _____

⟳ Equature

The specific incident which demonstrates today's performance in this area is: _____

_____

_____

_____

_____

The least acceptable area of performance today was in rating category number: _____

The specific incident which demonstrates today's performance in this area is: _____

_____

_____

_____

_____

Documentation of Performance and Comment:

Item #

_____	_____
_____	_____
_____	_____
_____	_____
_____	_____
_____	_____
_____	_____
_____	_____
_____	_____
_____	_____
_____	_____
_____	_____

_____   _____
Trainer's Signature   CTO's Signature

_____
CTO Supervisor's Signature

1. Set the Stage/Scene	4. Use Lists as Appropriate	7. Think Remedial	10. Don't Predict
2. Consider Verbatim Quotes	5. Report Facts/Avoid Conclusions	8. Quantify When Appropriate	
3. Critique Performance/Not the Person	6. Check Spelling/Grammar, Etc.	9. Remember Your Audience	

Appendix - 4

Daily Observation Report

Daily Observation Report

S Equature
BUILT TO SERVE PUBLIC SAFETY

Evaluation Date _____ Date Prepared _____

Evaluator: _____ ID# _____

Trainee: _____ ID # _____

Rating instructions: Circle the number on the scale that indicates the trainee's proficiency level of each task. Use the scale below. Document each item with comments for improvement, printouts of incidents and/or specific occurrence reports for ratings 1 through 3. Also attach commendation letters or comments that substantiate the scores given.

Rating scale: Not Acceptable: 1   Acceptable: 4   Superior: 7

General Topics

	1 2 3 4 5 6 7	N/O	NRT		RT
1	OOOOOOO	☐	☐	1. Attitude toward communications work	_____
2	OOOOOOO	☐	☐	2. Able to accept change/adjust to problems	_____
3	OOOOOOO	☐	☐	3. Accepts instruction/constructive criticism	_____
4	OOOOOOO	☐	☐	4. Works effectively with others	_____
5	OOOOOOO	☐	☐	5. Control of emotions/no hindrance to performance	_____

Telephone Responsibilities

	1 2 3 4 5 6 7				
6	OOOOOOO	☐	☐	6. Maintains patience and courtesy with the public	_____
7	OOOOOOO	☐	☐	7. Handles multiple incoming calls/multiple tasks	_____
8	OOOOOOO	☐	☐	8. Handles emotional/irate callers calmly	_____
9	OOOOOOO	☐	☐	9. Relates details given by callers	_____
10	OOOOOOO	☐	☐	10. Enters complete information about incidents	_____

Radio Responsibilities

	1 2 3 4 5 6 7				
11	OOOOOOO	☐	☐	11. Voice clarity and projection	_____
12	OOOOOOO	☐	☐	12. Assigns calls promptly and by priority	_____
13	OOOOOOO	☐	☐	13. Handles messages/requested service/multiple tasks	_____
14	OOOOOOO	☐	☐	14. Relays complete/accurate info on calls	_____
15	OOOOOOO	☐	☐	15. Uses codes and terminology correctly	_____
16	OOOOOOO	☐	☐	16. Hears and comprehends incoming radio traffic	_____

Miscellaneous Topics

	1 2 3 4 5 6 7				
17	OOOOOOO	☐	☐	17. Knowledge of city geography	_____
18	OOOOOOO	☐	☐	18. Officer/civilian safety incidents	_____
19	OOOOOOO	☐	☐	19. Knowledge of policies and procedures	_____
20	OOOOOOO	☐	☐	20. Adheres to policies and procedures	_____

_____ Total minutes of remedial training time

Appendix - 5

Daily Observation Report

The most satisfactory area of performance today was rating category number

A specific incident that demonstrates today's performance in this area is

The area of performance today that needs the most improvement was category number

Documentation of performance and comments:

Cat. #

_____	_____
_____	_____
_____	_____
_____	_____
_____	_____

Remedial training performed

Assignment

_____		_____	
Trainee	Date	CTO	Date
_____		_____	
Supervisor	Date	Training Supervisor	Date

Appendix - 6

REFERENCES

Alepidis, N. (2020, November 10). *Five Ways to Increase Wellbeing in the Workplace*. Motivirus. Retrieved August 29, 2022, from https://motivirus.com

Arun, T. (2021, December 28). *Busting the myths associated with employee training and development*. ZOHO. Retrieved November 30, 2022, from http://zoho.com

Bishop, D. (2022, December 7). *What Are Common Reasons to Work Overtime? (with pictures)*. Smart Capital Mind. Retrieved April 26, 2022, from https://www.smartcapitalmind.com/what-are-common-reasons-to-work-overtime.htm

Brady, S. (2022, January 12). *82% of Workers Would Consider Quitting Their Jobs Because of a Bad Manager*. ValuePenguin. Retrieved June 17, 2022, from https://www.valuepenguin.com/news/majority-workers-would-leave-job-becuase-of-manager

CALEA. (2022). *CALEA The Gold Standard in Public Safety.* Home | CALEA® | The Commission on Accreditation for Law Enforcement Agencies, Inc. Retrieved October 13, 2022, from https://calea.org/

Calvert, D. (2018, October 15). *How To Be A Successful First-Time Supervisor.* Leadership, Sales, and Teamwork Blog by People First Productivity Solutions. Retrieved August 26, 2022, from https://blog.peoplefirstps.com/connect2lead/first-time-supervisors-success

Craig, W. (2016, August 26). *How to Balance Scrutiny In The Workplace.* Forbes. Retrieved January 6, 2023, from https://www.forbes.com/sites/williamcraig/2016/08/26/how-to-balance-scrutiny-in-the-workplace/?sh=1528be80224c

Dean, M. M. (2021, September 5). *Police struggle to Hire Officers and 9-1-1 Dispatchers as Homicides and Shootings Increase.* The Philadelphia Inquirer. Retrieved April 01, 2022, from https://www.msn.com/en-

us/news/crime/police-struggle-to-hire-officers-and-911-
dispatchers-as-homicides-and-shootings-increase/ar-
AAO7m7w

EE Editors. (2019, October 19). *The Four States of Competence
Explained*. Examined Existence. Retrieved October 13,
2022, from https://examinedexistence.com/the-four-states-
of-competence-explained/

Finnegan, R. (2018). *How to Conduct Stay Interviews: 5 Key
Questions*. SHRM. Retrieved February 8, 2023, from
https://www.shrm.org/resourcesandtools/hr-
topics/employee-relations/pages/how-to-conduct-stay-
interviews-part-2.aspx

Gilbert, I. (2019, December 2). *Reducing 911 Dispatcher Burnout
& Turnover Through Behavioral Insights | by What Works
Cities | Medium*. What Works Cities. Retrieved March 25,
2022, from https://whatworkscities.medium.com/reducing-
911-dispatcher-burnout-through-behavioral-insights-
301726b80bce

Hannon, K. (2015, June 4). *Exit Interview Do's and Don'ts*.
Forbes. Retrieved February 3, 2023, from

https://www.forbes.com/sites/nextavenue/2015/06/04/exit-interview-dos-and-donts/?sh=7bf575e045fa

IAED. (2022). *Raise the Bar as an Accredited Center of Excellence*. International Academies of Emergency Dispatch. Retrieved October 13, 2022, from https://www.emergencydispatch.org/what-we-do/accreditation

Information Commissioner's Office. (n.d.). *Leadership and oversight*. ICO. Retrieved June 28, 2022, from https://ico.org.uk/about-the-ico/who-we-are/

The Investopedia Team. (2021, November 25). *How Much Should I Contribute to My 401(k)?* Investopedia. Retrieved March 21, 2021, from https://www.investopedia.com/articles/retirement/082716/your-401k-whats-ideal-contribution.asp

Kelly, E. L. (2020, February 18). *4 Reasons Employees Work Overtime & How HR Can Help - HR in ASIA*. HR in Asia. Retrieved April 26, 2022, from https://www.hrinasia.com/employee-relations/%ef%bb%bf4-reasons-employees-working-overtime/

Kraus, E. (2022, August 11). *How to Become a BBB Accredited Business in 3 Steps*. Fit Small Business. Retrieved October 17, 2022, from https://fitsmallbusiness.com/bbb-accredited/

Mehnert, D. (2012, October 4). *Standard Evaluation Guidelines*. Golden Police Department. Retrieved January 10, 2023, from https://www.bing.com/ck/a?!&&p=92da7e198fbc448bJmlt dHM9MTY3MzMwODgwMCZpZ3VpZD0yNTRjMzZiM i00YmQzLTY1MjEtMTE1OC0yNzc2NGE0MDY0OGU maW5zaWQ9NTI0NQ&ptn=3&hsh=3&fclid=254c36b2-4bd3-6521-1158-27764a40648e&psq=911+daily+observation+report+exam ples&u=a1aHR0cDovLzkxM

Liu, J. (2021, November 12). *The Great Resignation*. CNBC. Retrieved April 13, 2022, from https://www.cnbc.com/2021/11/12/a-record-4point4-million-people-quit-jobs-in-september-great-resignation.html

Maxwell, J. (2011, June 11). *Failing Forward - John Maxwell.*

Maxwell Leadership. Retrieved June 14, 2022, from

https://www.johnmaxwell.com/blog/failing-forward/

NENA. (2014). *NENA Standards & Other Documents.*

National Emergency Number Association. Retrieved

October 15, 2022, from

http://www.nena.org/page/Standards

Nguyen, S. (2010, May 03). *5 Reasons Why Employees Stay.* 5

Reasons Why Employees Stay. Retrieved April 13, 2022,

from https://www.workplacepsychology.net/2010/05/03/5-

reasons-why-employees-stay

Pannone, J. (2019, January 21). *What Makes Employees Stay - Top

10 Reasons Employers Should Know.* ForzaDash.

Retrieved April 13, 2022, from

https://www.forzadash.com/2019/01/21/what-makes-

employees-stay-top-10-reasons-employers-should-know/

Parker, K., & Menasce-Horowitz, J. (2022, March 9). *The Great

Resignation: Why workers say they quit jobs in 2021.* Pew

Research Center. Retrieved June 17, 2022, from

https://www.pewresearch.org/fact-

tank/2022/03/09/majority-of-workers-who-quit-a-job-in-

2021-cite-low-pay-no-opportunities-for-advancement-
feeling-disrespected/

Periyasamy, R. (2021, April 26). *7 Critical Employee Training
Issues - Solved with Apty*. Apty. Retrieved August 29,
2022, from https://www.apty.io/blog/employee-training-
issues-solved-with-apty

Prior, R. (2019, May 27). *Burnout is an official medical diagnosis,
World Health Organization says*. CNN. Retrieved July 13,
2023, from https://www.cnn.com/2019/05/27/health/who-
burnout-disease-trnd/index.html

Robbins, T., & Hariri, R. (2022). *Life Force: How New
Breakthroughs in Precision Medicine Can Transform the
Quality of Your Life & Those You Love*. Simon & Schuster.

Salary.com. (2022, 04 26). *911 Dispatcher Salary*. Salary.com.
Retrieved May 03, 2022, from
https://www.salary.com/research/salary/alternate/911-
dispatcher-salary

Siler, J. (2022, August 18). *Rethink Your College Degree
Requirements*. Forbes. Retrieved December 11, 2022, from
https://www.forbes.com/sites/forbeshumanresourcescounci

l/2022/08/18/rethink-your-college-degree-
requirements/?sh=6fccd36611cc

Slager, S. (2019, May 16). *Followership: A Valuable Skill No One Teaches*. Forbes. Retrieved January 6, 2023, from https://www.forbes.com/sites/forbesbostoncouncil/2019/05 /16/followership-a-valuable-skill-no-one-teaches/?sh=6f0758154695

Spain, E., & Groysberg, B. (2016, April). *Making Exit Interviews Count*. Harvard Business Review. Retrieved February 3, 2023, from https://hbr.org/2016/04/making-exit-interviews-count

Stromberg, J. (2014, December 15). *Lie detectors: Why they don't work, and why police use them anyway*. Vox. Retrieved April 21, 2022, from https://www.vox.com/2014/8/14/5999119/polygraphs-lie-detectors-do-they-work

Tremmaglia, M., & Harvey, B. (2022, January 21). *How to Get Recognition Right in 2022*. SHRM. Retrieved May 5, 2022, from https://www.shrm.org/learningandcareer/learning/webcasts /pages/0122tremmagliaharvey.aspx

References - viii

Tyler, K. (2021, October 5). *Stress management.* Mayo Clinic.

    Retrieved June 28, 2022, from

    https://www.mayoclinic.org/tests-procedures/stress-

    management/about/pac-20384898

United States Department of Labor. (1988, 01 01). *Employment*

    Law Guide - Law Detector Tests. United States

    Department of Labor. Retrieved April 21, 2022, from

    https://webapps.dol.gov/elaws/elg/eppa.htm?_ga=2.253495

    177.1083403201.1650547155-1988785460.1632406513

U.S. Department of Labor. (1993). *Family and Medical Leave*

    (FMLA). U.S. Department of Labor. Retrieved June 14,

    2022, from https://www.dol.gov/general/topic/benefits-

    leave/fmla

Vyvial, J. (2020, February 29). *4 Reasons Job Postings Don't List*

    Salary, And What to Do. FlexJobs. Retrieved May 21,

    2022, from https://www.flexjobs.com/blog/post/why-isnt-

    salary-always-listed-on-a-postin/

Walker, E. (2022, July 8). *Eight reasons for rising healthcare*

    costs. PeopleKeep. Retrieved November 14, 2022, from

    https://www.peoplekeep.com/blog/eight-reasons-for-

    rising-health-care-costs

Williams, J. (2022, February 23). *Phoenix Police Department Staffing and the Impact on Service to the Community.* City of Phoenix. Retrieved May 5, 2022, from https://www.phoenix.gov/policesite/Documents/Staffing%20Impact%20Report_Final.pdf

Wilson, M. (2022, January 5). *Modern Employee Recognition Programs & Trends for 2022.* Bucketlist Rewards. Retrieved May 5, 2022, from https://bucketlistrewards.com/blog/5-employee-recognition-trends-for-2022/